Sunday

MW01677508

A Time for Reflection

Questions Worth Asking
Stories to Live By
Journeys in Faith

Bill Smith

© 2009 Bill Smith
All Rights Reserved.

No part of this publication may be reproduced, stored in a retrieval system, or transmitted, in any form or by any means, electronic, mechanical, photocopying, recording, or otherwise, without the written permission of the author.

First published by Dog Ear Publishing
4010 W. 86th Street, Ste H
Indianapolis, IN 46268
www.dogearpublishing.net

dog ear PUBLISHING

ISBN: 978-160844-148-8

This paper is acid free and meets all ANSI standards for archival quality paper.
Printed in the United States of America

Table of Contents

Part I - A Look Back

Part II – Living in Today's World

Part III – Introducing Jesus

Acknowledgements

This collection of sermons began as a simple review of more than thirty years of preaching. My intent was first, to see in what ways my preaching may have evolved, and secondly, to leave my grandchildren something to add to their memory of "grandpa".

There are many persons who by their encouragement and support stand behind this book. Among those to whom I feel indebted are the congregations where these sermons were preached. By their patient listening, probing questions, and faithful response, these are the men, women, and children who let me know these sermons were, not only heard, but taken to heart and in many cases given flesh and blood. If these sermons have any power to inspire, these are the people who by their kind and gracious example inspired the author. To all of them I would like to express my deepest appreciation for the role they have played in enriching my life's journey.

Like any occupation, the role of the family in a minister's life is critical. To my wife, Patricia, whose life was more directly affected by these sermons than anyone will ever know, I am forever grateful for her support and feedback. She is the one whose Saturday nights and Sunday mornings were too often shaped by her husband's sermons, often hearing Sunday's sermon twice – once on Saturday and again Sunday morning. I owe many of the ideas in these sermons to her comments and suggestions, which helped keep them honest and grounded. Her technical assistance in putting this book together has been invaluable. And thanks to her photographic skills, the sun setting over the Pacific Ocean graces the book's cover.

When it comes to recognizing those who played a significant role in this book, I cannot forget the contributions of Mark and Jennifer, my son and daughter. Their "growing-up" years provided grist for many sermon illustrations, not all of which showed their father in a positive light. They not only paid the price of spending many quiet evenings upstairs in the parsonage while members of the new church start in Puyallup were meeting in the basement, but also let me know in a variety of ways that platitudes and pontificating were not helpful ways of communicating, and thus helped keep my sermons from becoming too "preachy".

I would also like to thank all those who helped get this book published. My son-in-law, Richard Hill, and my friends, James Davis and Flo Ariessohn, all read the manuscript and made insightful suggestions. Their encouragement and support along with all those people whose editing and marketing skills guided me through the publishing and production process have been of immense help during the writing of this book.

Like most preachers, the sermons we deliver are the product of thoughts that come from many sources. Events in our world and community, challenges our parishioners face, Biblical and contemporary authors, the morning newspaper, quiet times of prayer and meditation, and twinges of conscience that stir our compassion and concern for justice all play a role in keeping the "sermon pot" stirred. Hopefully, reading these sermons may stir thoughts and feelings for you, the reader, as well, and perhaps provide seeds for creating your own contribution to building a world where peace and justice may truly reign.

"Preaching: An Introduction"

"With his fabulous tale to proclaim, the preacher is called to stand in his pulpit as fabulist extraordinary, to tell the truth of the Gospel in its highest and wildest and holiest sense." Frederick Buechner

In many ways, the defining moment of my life as a pastor took place every Sunday morning when I stood before the congregation ready to deliver the sermon. It was here that members of the congregation, in all their various guises and roles, would gather, waiting to hear some word that might relieve their fears, revive their hopes, and strengthen their resolve. It was here that I was called to interpret the sacred scriptures so their power to heal, inspire, and challenge might truly touch the hearts and minds of all who sat before me.

Of all the tasks of ministry, preaching is perhaps the one place above all others where the pastor's role can most easily be described as "messenger for God". Acting in this capacity, I always felt was both a privilege and a great responsibility. It was a privilege bestowed by the church's history and tradition, assumed by the preacher's calling and ordination, and granted by the congregation. Where else do people come as a captive audience, listening to someone from whom they expect to hear the Word of God? To be responsible for proclaiming both God's truth and power so that it is relevant to people's lives is not something to take lightly, and I always felt both challenged and humbled by it.

The great German theologian, Karl Barth, once said that the preacher's task is to hold the daily newspaper in one hand and the Bible in the other, and show how the stories in each are related. Attempting to take this seriously, the focus of my preaching was generally more determined by the news of the day and things that happened in the lives of the congregation than the liturgical calendar. An exception was when I preached during the seasons of Advent and Lent, and the holy days of Christmas, Easter, and Pentecost. Most of the time, however, sermon topics centered on a personal or social issue.

It has been said that the preacher's task is to comfort the afflicted and afflict the comfortable - the former more likely occurring when the preacher assumes a pastoral role, the latter when his role is more prophetic. The danger with the prophetic type sermon is the preacher may separate him or herself from the congregation and pontificate, telling people where they have either failed or should change their ways. The danger with sermons of a more comforting nature is one may end up with platitudes that fail to take seriously the depth of a person's hurt and pain. Wanting to avoid both pontificating and the syrupy, sweetness of platitudes, I always tried to use "we" instead of "you", including myself with the congregation as the one to whom the sermon was addressed.

The sermons that follow are divided into three sections and grouped according to certain themes. The first section examines how we look at the world, and includes the first sermon preached in a new church, some questions worth asking, and some stories to live by. Section two is designed to help us determine what counts in coping with some of life's challenges. The third section introduces Jesus, asking what we may learn from his life as seen through the various roles he played. In each of these sections I have chosen sermons that may serve a devotional purpose and can, hopefully, inspire and encourage resolve in meeting today's challenging times.

"New Beginnings"

"I have learned one important thing in my life – how to begin again." Sam Keen

The first Sunday in a new church brings an abundance of questions and high hopes – all bundled with the preacher's nervous energy and the congregation's cautious judgment. Meeting for the first time, preacher and congregation size each other up, wondering how they will "hit it off" and if working together will be fun or a burden.

On six different occasions, I stood before a congregation to preach my first sermon. In 1969, it was an older congregation in the small town of Monroe, home of the Washington state reformatory. Two years later, the pulpit was half-way across the world in Wesley Church, Auckland, New Zealand, where I participated in a year-long, pulpit-exchange. The following year began a seven-year ministry at Green Lake, a neighborhood church in north Seattle. My final three "first Sundays" found me starting a new congregation on South Hill, Puyallup, in 1982; and serving two more, north-end Seattle churches – Woodland Park in 1992 and Sand Point in 1997.

While each of these "first" sermons focuses on the church's mission, there is an interesting shift in emphasis that takes place during the twenty-eight year span of time. The very first sermon, which was repeated both in Auckland and at Green Lake, asks, "What is it that we have in common?" and proceeds to describe, in light of the historical church, our "scope of responsibility", the nature of our "relationship with God", and our "assigned task". Here, the emphasis is on the historical church which belongs to Christ. We are members, but it is neither our creation nor possession. It dictates who we are, not vice-versa. The approach is not suggestive, what might we share, but rather descriptive; not what can we become, but who we already are and what we are called to do.

Starting the new church in Puyallup, the emphasis is no longer on the historical church, but building the "dream" church; no longer descriptive, but suggestive. Basing the dream on Christ's admonition to his disciples to be a "light to the world", different kinds of lights become symbols for the dream church's ministry – a "search" light with its focus on finding the world's lost and hurting; a "signal" light, providing guidance and direction; and a "reflector" light, reminding us we are dependent upon God and it is God's glory, not our own, that we seek.

At Woodland Park, the answer to "what we share" is no longer found in our dream church, but in Christ. It is our love for Christ and desire to emulate his love in the world that brings us together, not anything we may have in common as members of society. We may or may not share secular interests, but we do share our desire to follow Christ's way of love. Hence, our interdependence comes from and flows through Christ.

Coming to my last pulpit at Sand Point, my sermon focuses on the question, "What do we see?" Here, there is a shift in emphasis from the historical institution of the church as the basis for ministry to the way we look at the world and ourselves. This approach focuses on each church member, and using the stories of the Israelites spying out Canaan and the anointing of Jesus at Bethany, it asks which screens will filter our sight. Will it be those focusing on the obstacles we face, or those which look at our own resources? Will our filters be those complaining about what might have been, or those that are appreciative of what already is and open to see the gifts, talents, and divine possibilities so abundantly present in each of our fellow members?

"Our Common Journey"

If someone were to interrupt our service this morning and ask each of us, "What is it that we have in common?" what kind of answer would we give? Other than our common humanity, what are those things which we all share?

Living in a day of divisiveness and dissent, we may find it helpful to begin our ministry together by emphasizing our common heritage. Remembering something of our past can provide a focus for where we as a church go in the future. As members of Christ's church, we belong to one of the oldest institutions in society. In its present form the Christian church is over 2,000 years old; though its origins can be traced back nearly 4,000 years to the Israelite tribes. The church's history not only outdates any of us, but the birth of this nation as well. As Albert Barnett has noted, "Men (women) compose the membership of the church, but the church does not on that account belong to them. The church is Christ's; it is neither our creation nor our possession." We may have had a part in helping to provide a building where a part of the historical church has met, but no such building would be needed were it not for the life and death of that carpenter in Nazareth.

In light of this past history of the church, I would like to let us hear from two people who played a prominent role in the early life of the church. One was the prophet Isaiah and the other was one of its earliest converts – Paul. Together, they express three aspects of God's relationship to the church that we might hold up as our common heritage. The first is a definition of the scope of our responsibility; the second is the nature of our relationship to God; and the third assigns us a common task.

The scope of our responsibility as a church is as extensive as the needs of people. The prophet Isaiah, while reminding his fellow Israelites of God's faithfulness in preserving them as a people, startles them by saying something that is still revolutionary today. In the prophet's straight-forward manner, Isaiah proclaims, "It is too light a thing for Israel to be only a servant to her own people; God intends for us to be a light to all the nations so salvation might reach to the ends of the earth." Hence, Isaiah shifts the responsibility of the Israelites from their own nation, to every nation. No longer can they serve the Lord only among their own kind – such service is too narrow and limiting. Those who will serve the Lord must be a light to all people. No national boundary (Gentile or Jew); no single color (red, yellow, black, brown, or white); no one denomination (Methodist, Baptist, Lutheran) must stand outside the responsibility of those people who would serve God. Our vision must be global even while our action is local for no community in the world today exists in isolation.

Since the scope of our responsibility as a church is global, our membership is all-inclusive. Being a voluntary organization, the church is one of the few institutions in our society with no discriminatory membership restrictions – persons of any age, race, nation, social class, or educational background may join. Knowing this, however, we in the church have not always lived up to it. As a result, many critics have taken great delight in pointing out the rigid social stratification that characterizes much of the church's life.

If we are to answer these critics, we must remember that as a church the scope of our responsibility calls us to tear down all fences that separate people. If we are to serve God faithfully, we must be a light to all people; not just our fellow church members or white Americans. (fellow Kiwis when in New Zealand)

A second aspect of our common heritage, and the most basic, concerns the nature of our relationship to God. Revealing his nature to us in the life of Christ, God comes to us in human form. Through Christ, God changes the very nature of our relationship. Like the sun coming out on a foggy day, God lifts the veil that prevents us from seeing him clearly, coming to us at those points where we live out our lives. As we yearn to be free, Christ comes to us as one who is in bondage to no one. As we yearn for peace, Christ comes to us as one who even in the face of death is able to say, "Not my will, but thine be done." As we feel the burden of past mistakes, Christ comes as one who says, "Pick up your bed and walk...your sins are forgiven...go and sin no more." As we find it far easier to condemn than to forgive, Christ comes as one who says, "Let him who is without sin cast the first stone." Where once God was hidden, God is now revealed. Where once we felt estrangement and confusion, we now know the depth of God's love and acceptance. Where once we were no people, now we are God's people. As Paul writes in his letter to the Corinthians, "God has reconciled us men (and women) to himself through Christ."

Yet, it is at this very point of reconciliation and a new relationship to God that many of our churches have fallen short. The theologian, Robert Cushman, expresses it this way, "Christian churches have cut-short the working spirit of the living Christ because they have understood reconciliation as forgiveness of sins but have forgotten that it also means newness of life." God has not only accepted us; God has restored us for life. We are free to celebrate life and to rejoice in it. To be the people of God is a serious calling, but it surely does not mean that we must lose our sense of joy and laughter.

Hence, the second aspect of our common heritage concerns the changed nature of our relationship to God. He comes to us in Christ as the One who breaks down our fears, egoism, and hostility that separate us from Him and from each other. He frees us from our distrust of the unknown that we may be open to the future and to one another. As one of Peter Marshall's prayers phrases it, "We may not know what the future holds, but we know who holds the future." Because it is God's grace that controls the course of our history, we can live each day with a sense of boldness and quiet confidence.

The third and final aspect of our common heritage is enlistment in a common task. Having been given our true humanity from God, we are now called to see that others who are in bondage are also set free. If we are free men and women, then we must free others. If we are forgiven, then we must forgive others. If we have been given new sight, then we must share our vision with our neighbors.

While the church is a human institution and therefore subject to all the imperfections of any other organized human effort, the church is always more than an institution of society. It is also an outpost of God, and is therefore called to extend God's rule in history. Hence, as members of the church we are not governed by society's norms and answerable to society's pressures. As long as Jesus is our Lord, it is to him and his teachings that we must be obedient.

Looking to the life of Christ we can see that the task of the church today is to be with God in the midst of the world's needs. As our Bishop Maynard Sparks said at Annual Conference, "The church is the only institution in our society more concerned about those on the outside than those within." If we are to be faithful to the living God we serve, then we must see that his spirit of love and justice is active in our community as well as in the church.

This means that as a church we will be present in the life of Monroe, affirming those forces that permit men and women to be human and seeking to overcome those antagonisms and divisions leading to disunity and injustice. As agents of reconciliation we will inevitably find ourselves involved in conflict since the commitment of reconciliation is to face and resolve conflicts, not escape them. It was this kind of commitment that led Christ to the cross and it is this kind of commitment that has led Christian martyrs ever since to their death. Few, if any of us, will ever be called to die in serving God, but we should remember that the life after which the church is patterned did not die a peaceful death.

In his final charge to ministers at Annual Conference, Bishop Sparks related a newspaper story that his son sent him. It told of a trial that had taken place in which the family of a man who had been killed in a train accident was suing the railroad for damages. In the course of the trial the signal man for the railroad was called to testify. The prosecuting attorney asked him if he had seen the accident, and he replied that he had. He was then asked if he had swung his lantern to warn the approaching car, and again he said "yes". As a result, the damage suit was not allowed. A few days later, the railroad president called and told him thanks – he had saved the company a lot of money. With a sigh of relief, the signal man confided that he was happy the trial was over. Not entirely understanding, the president asked, "Didn't you swing the lantern?" "Yes," the signal man answered, "but I was afraid he would ask me if it was lit – the wind had blown it out."

Like the signal man, we in the church have a responsibility to bear light to those traveling in darkness. But we must see to it that the lanterns we wave have not gone out. If we are to be faithful witnesses to God's light, then we must preserve our common heritage, remembering that (1) the scope of our responsibility is to all people, (2) we have been forgiven and restored for life through Christ, and (3) we have been called to a common task – serving as agents of reconciliation to overcome those barriers that separate men and women from each other and from their true humanity. If we in the church ever lose an over-powering sense of mission to the world as our very reason for existence, then we will have lost our definitive nature as the servants of God, the body of Christ, and the communion of the Holy Spirit. In our effort to be that kind of church, Pat and I look forward to sharing with you our common heritage and ministry.

"Building the Dream"

"They were dreamers like you. They carried a world-picture in their breast, of which they wanted to know the meaning. They were powerless against the world, yet they are the torch-bearers in the procession of human kind; and it is owing to them that there is not night over the earth." Thus, Johan Bojer, the great Norwegian writer, describes those persons whose lives have helped shape our world.

This morning we too are dreamers; we dream about our hopes for this church, whose very name, Light of the Hill, connotes a dream – a dream that is grounded in Jesus' call to his disciples, "You are the light of the world…let your light so shine before men, that they may see your good works, and give glory to your Father in heaven."

What might it mean for us to fulfill such a dream – to truly be a "light" on South Hill that brings to all people a sense of God's presence – a presence that is both comforting and inspiring. Let me begin by suggesting three kinds of light that might enable us to become such a "life-giving" light.

The first kind of light is a "<u>search</u>" light – a light whose focus is on the world. As that well-known scripture, John 3:16, makes abundantly clear, "God so loves the <u>world</u> that he gives his only son." God's love is not only for the church, but it is meant for <u>all the world</u>. Indeed, the church's uniqueness among human institutions is that it is the only one more concerned about those on the outside than those within. Its purpose is to serve others; to seek the lost, the hurt, and the broken wherever they are.

Loren Eiseley, one of my favorite authors, tells the story in his book, <u>The Unexpected Universe</u>, of a man he once observed picking up a starfish on the beach. When Eiseley asked, "Are you a collector?" the man replied, "No," and with a quick, gentle movement swung the starfish over his head and far out to sea. "It may live," he said, "if the offshore pull is strong enough." Later that night, Eiseley reflected that the star-thrower was just one man and death was running more swiftly than he along every beach in the world. Yet, several days later as he walked that same beach, he too picked up a starfish and found himself emulating the star-hurlers actions with the thought, "He and I are not alone, after us there will be others." Like the star-thrower, we too are called to reach out against all odds, and give someone another chance.

Is this not one of the reasons Christ is so compelling – like the star-thrower his compassion is not overwhelmed by the enormity of the task. His concern for the least, illustrated by his story about the shepherd who leaves the ninety nine sheep to go out and search for the one that is lost, doesn't seem to make sense, but his arithmetic is not always like ours; the bottom line for Jesus never loses sight of the one who is lost.

One last comment about reaching out to those in need – when doing so, it is important that we not only treat the hurt, but that we also work to fix the cause. It's important to see that the accident victim is taken to the hospital, but it's just as important to fix the road that caused the accident. If the church is to play a healing role in an individual's life, it must also seek to address the underlying problems that may contribute to that person's illness. Feeding the hungry is good, but providing a good education, job training, and a living wage are equally important.

The second kind of light that brings life to the world is a "signal" light. Signal lights protect and give direction for movement to people at cross-roads. As a signal light, the church is called to provide guidance and direction to help people clarify their values and make good decisions. A sound Christian education is a life-long process, which means Sunday school is not just for kids; whether it's on Sunday or any other day, the church's education program needs to include adults of all ages. Further more, a good Christian education program should be well balanced, providing opportunities for personal growth and family needs such as money management, conflict resolution, marriage enrichment, and parenting classes as well as Bible study and classes dealing with social and justice issues such as racism, housing, hunger, homelessness, and stewardship of the environment.

To be an effective "signal" light the church must insure teachers are well trained and quality education materials are available, but it must also pay attention to its own primary signal light – the carpenter from Nazareth. He is the one who teaches us how we are to embody the love of God and the kind of light we are to shed. He comes to us at those points where we live out our lives. As we yearn for peace, Christ comes to us as one who gives us peace this world can neither give nor take away; as we feel the burden of past mistakes, Christ comes to say, "Pick up your bed and walk…your sins are forgiven…go and sin no more." When we are greedy to be #1, we see him stoop to wash his disciples' feet; and when we find it easier to condemn than forgive, Christ comes to say, "Let that one of you without sin, cast the first stone."

The third kind of light that can help us be a "light on the hill" is a "reflector" light. Just as the stain-glass window only shows its true beauty when it reflects the sun, so must the church reflect God's son. Being a reflector reminds us who we are dependent upon and to whom we owe our light. The church's purpose in doing good works is not to glorify itself, but the God it seeks to serve. Such awareness is seen by Jesus' response when a man, asking what he must do to inherit eternal life, addresses him as "Good Master." "Why do you call me good," Jesus responds, "No one is good but God alone." Before he has anything to say about eternal life, Jesus reminds the man, and us, that only our Creator and Sustainer is truly good.

When we are truly a reflector light, we think not in terms of what we have done, but rather in terms of what God has enabled us to do. I pray that whatever success we may achieve in bringing light to the world, whatever comfort and healing we may provide, whatever guidance and wisdom we may offer, we never forget the One who gives us the energy and direction to provide it. We are called to be Christ's ambassadors, and it is in his name that we live and serve.

A story is told about an Australian bush preacher who serves three different churches in the outback. As he arrives at the last one, it is beginning to get dark. In the distance, he sees lights flickering in the bush. As he gets nearer the church, he discovers the flickering lights are hurricane lamps being carried to the service by members of the congregation.

Though they are not hurricane lamps, when we entered here this morning, each of us received a candle. At the conclusion of our service, I will light the Christ candle on our altar and our ushers will use it to light their own candles. They will, in turn, pass up each aisle, lighting the candles of those persons nearest the aisle. Each one of you will receive light for your candle from the person sitting beside you, and then you in turn may offer light to your neighbor. At the end of our service, you are invited to carry this light of Christ into the world, remembering as you go that Christ, not only calls us to be a light for all the world, but it is his light that always goes before us. Thanks be to God. Amen.

The Journey of Faith

It is early November, 1982. In five days we will hold our very first worship service. The Puyallup School District has agreed to let us meet at the Ridgecrest Elementary School, where our daughter Jennifer is a third grader. A direct mailing has been sent to some five-thousand homes in our zip code area. We've advertised in our local newspaper, the Puyallup Herald, and contacted other United Methodist churches in our district, asking them to send a representative and bring a church banner.

As Sunday approaches, our excitement grows. For four months, a fifteen-member, steering committee has been preparing. In July, thirty-six persons attended a "Get-Acquainted" dessert in the parsonage; in August, more than sixty people found their way to Wildwood Park for a picnic and children's games; in September, we covered the walls of the parsonage basement with potential names before deciding to name our yet-to-be-born church, "Light of the Hill"; and in October, we compiled a list of seventy-three phone numbers of persons who had shown interest and invited them to a Halloween Party.

Now it is November, and time to take care of last-minute details. We borrow hymnals from as far away as Marysville, and pick up candles from Kauffer's, the Catholic book store in Seattle. Colby United Methodist Church brings us some old choir robes, and a variety of people contribute nursery cribs, offering plates, road signs, and a pulpit lectern. Greeters, ushers, and a pianist are lined up, and a sense of expectancy fills the air as we await Sunday morning.

The night before, I wonder how many will come, worry if we'll have enough hymnals, and pray that our visitors will be inspired. I write and re-write the sermon, hope for good weather in the morning, and try to get a good night's sleep.

Sunday morning is a bee-hive of activity. Folding chairs and tables are set up, banners are hung, refreshments are set out for the coffee hour after the service. Then, we hold our breath to see who will come. Moments later, a steady stream of people passing through the gymnasium necessitates opening the partition doors that divide the gym in half – doors we had earlier closed to make the setting more intimate.

Powerful feelings, so abundantly present at that first worship service, have been repeated many times in the ensuing five years: feelings of euphoria on that first Easter when one-hundred-twenty-seven persons lit candles symbolizing their desire to become charter members; feelings of anxiety when we learn Paine Field's flight pattern for landings will come directly over the property where we plan to build our church, and feelings of uncertainty when we spend the next several months selling our original church site and buying another; feelings of sadness as Bill and Jeannie Gloss announce their move to California – a move followed in ensuing months by numerous other church families; feelings of sympathy and grief as we sit with Beryl and Clint and Mike March's mother, grieving their loss; feelings of disappointment when the early excitement of some members wanes and they choose to leave.

We've seen people come and go: 403 have joined the church, 92 have moved, 6 have died, and 38 have transferred their membership elsewhere. Sometimes they have left with tears and sad "goodbyes"; sometimes they've just seemed to disappear without a word and we were left to wonder why. We've laughed – remember the children's talk when I asked if anyone knew a grumpy person and little Mark Berger said, "Yea, my dad"; we've loved – how can I forget the time four-year old Josh Smith came running up to me in the grocery store, gave me a big hug, and said, "I haven't seen you in a hundred years"; we've listened, worried, and disagreed deciding where to re-locate after we sold our original five acres; and we've prayed and waited as we watched this building slowly being built and waited for the rains to stop so we could pave the parking lot.

Through it all, we've grown! Moving from the school to our beautiful first unit (our eventual sanctuary and additional classrooms will come later); moving from full conference financial support to being financially independent; moving from a first-year budget of $18,000 to a $90,000 budget next year. And how can we measure how we've grown as people of faith? DARING TO RISK UNCOMFORTABLE INVOLVEMENTS – visiting the sick and dying, inviting strangers to church, speaking out against social injustices; giving ten per cent of our income to feed the hungry and help provide for the homeless; LETTING GO OF SOME OF OUR FEARS – Can we appeal to young families just starting out and be financially viable? Will people be able to find where we worship? (I nearly got lost picking up my daughter after the first day of school) Will we be able to sell the original five acres and find a good location for a new site? ALLOWING OURSELVES TO BE VULNERABLE – Admitting our mistakes (reporting to authorities the birthmarks of an Asian baby we're caring for in our nursery appear to be signs of child abuse), acknowledging our doubts (sponsoring a peace forum in a military environment), and openly dealing with prejudices (inviting a gay priest to speak and our subsequent involvement with AIDS).

Some of you may have attended our first worship service and remember the sermon that day. Who am I kidding? It was entitled, "Building the Dream". As we gather here five years later, reflecting on our journey of faith, we may do well to ask ourselves again, "What is the dream we are building?" If it is only numerical growth and our own success, surely we will fail. But if as Paul's letter to those early Christians at Ephesus suggests, it is to open our hearts and minds to God's love and bend our wills to God's purposes, then perhaps our continuing journey of faith can help build the dream that the Christian church has shared through the centuries – that all the kingdoms of this world shall be one and God's peace and justice will reign in the hearts of all.

After my first year in seminary, I spent the summer working with the National Parks ministry in Yosemite. At the end of the summer, I took the train from San Francisco back to New Haven. Sitting next to me was a young, Chinese women going back to Harvard where she had just won a scholarship. Though I have long forgotten her name, I can't forget the intensity of the dream she shared; it was a dream of building a bridge between the East and the West to help bring peace to the world.

Our joining the church is like getting on a train. It doesn't matter when we get on or off, or even where we go; what matters is the dreams we share, the people we touch, and in the midst of our sharing, catching a glimpse of God working in our lives. In the end, may we become a little better people – more compassionate, more concerned about others, more willing to forgive, and a little closer to the dream of new creation God intends for us all. And may all those with whom we share this journey come to discover a sense of God's presence, not only working in us, but stirring in their own lives as well. When God's grace comes along for the ride, there is no telling how far we will go, nor where we may end up.

"Declaring Our Inter-Dependence"

Doris sits nervously waiting. It is ten minutes before three – ten minutes before she will meet her twin brother whom she hasn't seen in forty years. They have been separated since birth. What will he look like? Will they have anything in common? How will they hit it off?

Doris' story is also our story. We too are meeting for the first time. We too are filled with questions, wondering about our relationship – how we will hit it off? How we will work together? Will we meet or fail to meet each other's expectations? This morning my face and voice are strange to most of you; our past histories are unknown to each other, but we do not meet in a vacuum.

Like Doris and her twin brother, even though we are strangers, we are already related. As Paul reminds us, the basis of our relationship is not who we are in ourselves, but who we are in Christ. The difference is important to keep in mind because it has everything to do with how we relate.

In ourselves, we are quite different. Some of us are extroverts, finding crowds and conversation easy, and some of us are introverts, much more comfortable in quiet one-on-one settings. Some of you will share my interest in sports - maybe some of you are even fellow Jayhawks; others don't even know the name of the local sports teams and can care less. Some of you may, like Pat and me, be movie buffs who have our favorite actor and actresses and look forward to their next picture; others of you prefer different forms of entertainment. Some of you have traveled extensively, and like Pat, hardly come home from one trip before you are already planning the next one; others are quite content to live in Seattle and gladly stay home.

In our relationship that is grounded in Christ, however, we are brothers and sisters who have much in common. Together, we seek to follow the ways of Jesus, welcoming strangers, visiting the sick, comforting the dying, forgiving our enemies, and attempting to manifest the Christian virtues of patience, forbearance, love, and servanthood. As the great German theologian Dietrich Bonhoeffer has written, "We are not in the church because we love each other; what we love is Christ and his way."

A number of years ago, when I was living in Bloomington, Indiana, the church council wanted to improve race relations in the city, and encouraged churches to engage in dialogue with those of different ethnic backgrounds. Taking it seriously, the minister of a white, middle-class, suburban church and the minister of a black, inner-city church who knew each other from their seminary days, decided they would bring their two congregations together over a potluck, hoping this would enable people to get to know each other as individuals. The night of the gathering, people were asked to introduce themselves to the group, but as people did so their differences in background became not only obvious, but somewhat of a distancing factor. The economic differences along with the very different educational opportunities the two groups had experienced soon made every one feel uncomfortable and embarrassed.

At this point, wanting to change the atmosphere, the minister of the inner city church stood up and suggested every one introduce him or her self by talking about their faith – how they had become involved in the church and what difference it had made in their lives. Subsequently, the whole tenor of the evening changed; their differences were no longer so glaring and the common faith they shared brought a new appreciation and respect for each other.

When the source of our community is found merely in relation to each other apart from our faith, the emphasis is on status - our income, education, the home we live in, and the car we drive. But when we see each other as fellow Christians, we stand with each other as forgiven sinners called by God to use our compassion and love to help bring healing and social justice to the world. As Frederick Buechner, one of this country's great preachers and Christian writers, has said, "Our community in the church is not derived from choosing to be with those we like, but being with those who like Christ." When we love for Christ's sake, loyalty to one another is not a matter of who we like, but who Christ likes.

When William Temple was Archbishop of Canterbury during World War II, he would spend a part of each afternoon walking through the war torn neighborhoods, offering whatever help the church might provide. One afternoon, while visiting one of the bombed out sections of London, he came upon a group of boys playing stick ball in the street. Thinking he would have some fun with them, he asked, "I'll bet you boys don't know who I am?" One of the young lads, seeing the Archbishop's royal robes and sensing a bit of arrogance in the question, quickly replied, "Yes, I do. Mister, you're a miserable sinner." That evening the Archbishop wrote in his diary, "Today I learned what Jesus meant when he said, except you become like a little child, you shall not enter the kingdom of God."

Yesterday we celebrated another 4th of July – a time to remember our independence as a country. There is an appropriate time for all of us to stand alone and discover our identity as individuals. Self-reliance is a virtue to be admired. But as important as it is for us to declare our independence, it is just as important to declare our interdependence – to remind ourselves we are all members of the body of Christ, each bringing gifts crucial for our survival and growth.

As we receive communion this morning, we are all drawn to a central focus: the life of Christ that has been poured out for us all as an expression of God's love, and a reminder that our community as Christians comes from God. Its foundation and strength lie in the one whom we seek to follow, in whose name we gather, and whose body we share.

In the name of Christ, let us begin our ministry together. Reaching out to the hurt, brokenness, and hopelessness of the world, our mission is to bring healing and reconciliation. In the days ahead, as we come to understand and be understood by each other, may we grow in our fellowship and care for one another. For now, we come as strangers, but we also come as friends who have a common fellowship in Christ. Building upon the foundation that Christ has laid, let us join hands and begin together a new chapter in our journey of faith.

Glory to God, world without end. Amen.

"The Eyes That See"

Last September, I stood in the SeaTac baggage claim area, awaiting the arrival of a political science professor and his wife from Norway. Through the University of Washington's housing office, Pat and I had arranged for them to stay in our home while we spent a year in Romania – Pat teaching political science at Babes-Bolyai University in Cluz and me teaching English as a second language at a high school in Beclean. I had never met our house sitters before so we had brought along a sign with their names and held it up for them to see. As we waited, my mind played on the keyboard of possibilities What will they look like? Why didn't we exchange photographs? How will we relate? How will they care for our home?

This morning as we meet for the first time, we too can play that keyboard of possibilities. What kind of preacher will he be? How will he like our church? Will we work well together? What kind of ministry will we share?

This morning's biblical texts offer an interesting screen for our viewing. The Old Testament account of Moses sending the twelve spies into Canaan is a familiar story to many of us. The twelve men, each representing a different tribe of Israel, are instructed to find out how habitable the land is, what sort of people live there, and what kind of crops are raised. In addition, they are asked to bring back some of the produce they find.

Upon their return, the spies display the grapes, figs, and pomegranates they have brought back and report that the land is indeed flowing with milk and honey. But they also report that the inhabitants are people of enormous size – so big in fact, that "we felt like grasshoppers in comparison," and they conclude their report, saying, "We cannot attack these people; they are stronger than us," and then further describe the country, adding, "it is a country that devours its inhabitants."

Hearing this, the Israelites are discouraged, but one of the spies named Caleb stands up, calls the people to silence, and says, "We must march in immediately and take the land; we are well able to conquer its inhabitants." Unfortunately, only one other spy agrees with Caleb's assessment; the other ten are filled with doubt. The difference of opinion centers around what the spies choose to look at – those who doubt the wisdom of entering the land, focus on what lays <u>before</u> <u>them</u>; those who are in favor of invading the land, focus on what lays <u>within</u> <u>them</u>. Ten look at the strength of the enemy; the other two look at their own strength.

Which screen will filter our sight as we enter into our ministry together? Will we look primarily at the challenges we face, or the resources we share? Will we focus more on the problems we may encounter, or the opportunities that are before us? I dare say, the success of our ministry will have more to do with how we share our gifts and talents than the size or difficulty of the problems we encounter.

Our New Testament story involves the anointing of Jesus at Bethany. While Jesus is visiting in the home of a man named Simon, a woman comes in with an alabaster jar of nard, very costly ointment. She then breaks the jar, and pours the ointment on Jesus' head. Some of those present were indignant, and complained that the ointment could have been sold for over three hundred denarii. This was indeed a considerable sum since one denarii was the equivalent of the day's wage of an unskilled laborer.

But Jesus defends the woman's actions, telling them to leave her alone, saying, "What she has done is a good thing…she has done what she could, anointing my body beforehand for its burial….where the gospel is proclaimed, what she has done will be told in remembrance of her."

Those who are indignant complain because their focus is on <u>what might have been</u>. In their mind, a better use would have been to sell the perfume and give the money to the poor. But Jesus sees what she has done as a good thing because his focus is not on what might have been, but rather <u>what is</u>. Jesus sees that the woman is acting out of compassion, and in his eyes her act of mercy is to be commended, not denigrated. One way of seeing, builds the woman up; the other, tears her down. There's little doubt which way of seeing, she prefers.

In our ministry, where will we focus? Will we see only what might have been, like the parent who complains that her daughter's report card could have had all "A's" if it weren't for the one "B", or will we congratulate her for an outstanding achievement? Will we be building each other up by seeing and celebrating the good we accomplish, or will we complain about what might have been had we only used a different approach?

Theophane the Monk, in his delightful, little book, "Tales of a Magic Monastery", tells a wonderful story about a monastery that has fallen on hard times. Once a great order, there now are only five monks left in the decaying chapel; the abbot and four others, all over seventy years old. Clearly it is a dying order.

In the deep woods surrounding the monastery there is a little hut that a rabbi from a nearby town occasionally uses for a retreat. As the abbot agonizes over the dying order, it occurs to him during one of the rabbi's retreats to call on him and ask if he can offer any advice that might save the monastery.

The rabbi welcomes the abbot, but when the abbot explains the purpose of his visit, the rabbi can only commiserate with him. "I know how it is," he says, "the spirit has gone out of the people. It is the same in my town. Almost no one comes to the synagogue anymore." So the two old men weep together. Then they read parts of the Torah and quietly pray. Before the abbot departs, they embrace one another, "It has been a wonderful thing that we should meet after all these years," the abbot says, but I have failed in my purpose for coming here. Is there nothing you can tell me, any piece of advice you can give that will help save our dying order?" "No, I am sorry," the rabbi responds. "I have no advice to give; the only thing I can tell you is that the Messiah is one of you."

When the abbot returns to the monastery, his fellow monks gather round and ask, "Well, what did the rabbi say?" "He couldn't help," the abbot answered. "We just wept and read the Torah together. But as I was leaving, he did say something rather strange. He said the Messiah is one of us. I don't know what he means."

In the days and weeks that follow, the monks ponder the rabbi's words and wonder if there is any possible significance. *The Messiah is one of us? Could he possibly have meant one of us monks? If he meant anyone, he probably meant Father Abbot. He has been our leader and is a man of prayer. On the other hand, he might have meant Brother Thomas; certainly Brother Thomas is a holy man. Everyone knows that Brother Thomas is a man of light. But what about Brother Elred? No, he certainly could not have meant Brother Elred! Elred gets crotchety at times. But come to think of it, even though he is difficult to live with, Elred is nearly always right. Often, very right. Maybe the rabbi did mean Brother Elred. But surely not Brother Phillip. Phillip is so passive, a real nobody. But then, when you think about it, he has a gift for always being there when you need him. He just seems to magically appear by your side. Maybe Phillip is the Messiah. Of course, the rabbi didn't mean me. He couldn't possibly have meant me. I'm just an ordinary person. Yet, supposing he did? Suppose I am the Messiah?* As they contemplate these thoughts, the old monks begin to treat each other with extraordinary respect on the off chance that one of them might indeed be the Messiah.

Because the monastery is surrounded by a beautiful forest, people still occasionally come to picnic on its tiny lawn and wander along some of its paths. As they do so, they sense this aura of extraordinary respect that surrounds the five old monks; a respect that seems to permeate the atmosphere of the place. There is something strangely compelling, even attractive, about it. Hardly knowing why, people begin to come back to the monastery more frequently, and not just to picnic. Sometimes they wander into the chapel to meditate and pray. They begin to bring their friends to show them this special place, and their friends, bring their friends.

In time, some of the visitors begin to enquire if they might join the monks in looking after the grounds and perhaps, putting a new roof on the chapel. After a while, one man asks, if he can join their order. In the following months, one by one, others ask if they too might join, and within a few years, the monastery once again becomes a thriving order, and thanks to the rabbi's gift, a vibrant center of light and spirituality.

As we reflect on the stories we have heard this morning, the outcome of each of them centers around the viewing screen. The majority of those sent to spy out Canaan choose to focus on the obstacles that might be encountered, but the two who bring an alternative vision focus on the resources within themselves. Similarly, those people who condemn the woman's gift of expensive perfume choose to see it in a negative light; they focus on what might have been a better use, but Jesus sees her actions through a softer filter of compassion. And finally, in the last story, the monastery regains its former glory when the monks who live there look at each other in a new way, seeing the divine possibilities in each other.

Which filter will we use as we begin our journey of faith together? Will we see only the problems and difficulties we may encounter, or the resources and strengths we each possess? Will we see our individual contributions with a critical eye, wondering how things might have been done differently, or will we focus with an appreciative eye on what already exists? If we truly see each other in the light of our divine possibilities, we may not only be surprised by what we accomplish, we may come to see the Messiah who lives among us still. Thanks be to God; world without end. Amen.

"Questions Worth Asking"

"Judge a man by his questions rather than his answers."
Voltaire

Some questions may be answered with a quantifiable number, a geographical name, or a set of directions. But other questions, especially those that are more philosophical, cannot be answered by a simple "yes" or "no" and do not necessarily have one "right" answer. What is the capital of Washington is an easy question to grade in a fifth grade geography test. But asking how much is enough or what is the value of prayer are not questions that have one correct answer. While answers to these later questions may vary widely, they are nonetheless important questions to ask.

When we ask how much is enough, seeking an answer only raises more questions: What is involved in learning to be content with what we have? Is our sense of well-being always dependent upon something outside of ourselves? To what extent does our sense of security depend upon having "more"? When does our desire for "more" become greed? What difference might it make to see ourselves as stewards whose primary responsibility is to care for what we have received rather than owners whose main concern is not only to keep what we have, but to acquire more?

Perhaps, a more theological question worth asking is, "Does prayer change anything?" Do our prayers always bring our hoped for results, or are they merely words and hopes cast into a void? The outcome of our prayers seems to depend, not only on what we ask, but also on the kind of God to whom we pray. Are we merely asking to have our fears removed and our desires satisfied, or are we asking what God wants – not only for us, but from us? Is God simply a celestial bellhop granting whatever we desire, or is God more concerned about the kind of person we become?

Christians are sometimes characterized as followers of Christ. But while this may be a relatively easy way of naming those who claim to be Christian, what is not so easy is determining what exactly it means to be such a follower. Who is this one whom we follow? What knowledge or disciplines may be required for those who seek to walk in this way? Where and how far will we be asked to go, and what may we need for the journey? What is our goal and what may be required in achieving it? In the end, will there be a reward, and will it be worth the cost?

One of the great mysteries of human life is the suffering of good and innocent people. Why a good God allows bad things to happen to the

"Jobs" of the world is a question that has troubled theologians throughout history. Does it matter whether God's role is active or passive – whether God <u>wills</u> such suffering or merely <u>allows</u> it? What role do we humans play in the suffering of innocent people? Does morality have anything to do with human suffering, or is suffering just the luck of the draw – something that can happen to anyone at anytime? Does the way we respond to tragedy make a difference? Can anything good come out of the suffering of innocent people?

While there are many more questions that are troubling and well worth our asking, these four can start the process. Hopefully, the questions raised in these sermons may stimulate our thinking, strengthen our faith, and provide some footholds for further exploration and thought.

How Much Is Enough?

Several years ago while teaching some seventh-graders, I asked them to identify the fifty states on a map and name their capitals. A hand in the back shot up, and upon being recognized, one of the better students asked, "How much do I need to know to get an "A"?

"How much is enough?" is a question we raise, not just in terms of a school exam, but throughout life. How much money will be enough to send the kids to college? If I get that position, will the salary be enough? How much must I save so I can retire? How much must we sell the house for in order to move into a condo or retirement home? How much exercise is enough to keep my blood sugar level low enough to avoid becoming diabetic?

Underlying the question, "How much is enough?" is often the feeling that we must always have more. This insatiable desire to have more has many faces. Its object is often money, but it may also be the desire to own more things – more furniture, more toys, more clothes, a bigger boat, a newer car; or it may be a desire for more status – more recognition, respect, and consideration. And in some cases, it may be a desire for more control; to be "numero uno" – the one who calls the shots.

Throughout life we study and work, invest and save, buy and sell, hoping we can one day say, "We have all we need." But do we ever really stop wanting more? Will we ever truly have enough? When we get to the top of the hill, isn't there always another hill to climb?

Perhaps, the theologian Jay Williams is right when he observes, "Our always wanting more is the way in which we clumsily express our intuition that we were made for what is endless and without bounds." But if this is true, does it mean only such a God can satisfy our desire for more? And if only that One who is eternal can relieve us of our desire for more, how can we live our lives so this becomes a reality?

This morning's parable in Luke's gospel is an appropriate story in this regard. The farmer's harvest seems sufficient for all his needs. The rains come just at the right time, there is no insect infestation, and the yield exceeds anything he can ever remember. This is indeed a "dream come true"; finally, he has hit the jackpot. His hard work has paid off, and at last he can be fully compensated for his efforts.

His only problem is finding sufficient storage space for the harvest. He thinks if he tears down his old barns and builds bigger ones, he can store enough grain for the future that he can take it easy and truly enjoy life. But the plan is barely formulated when God says to him, "You fool, this very night you must surrender your life; you've made your money – who will get it now?"

Some people hear this parable and wonder if God has an anti-rich bias. "What kind of God is it," they ask, "who treats such a hard worker's success with so little respect?" Is it wrong to work so hard, and want to relax and enjoy life?

Most commentaries, however, suggest the problem is not in God, but in the man. It's not that he poorly manages success; after all, tearing down old barns and building bigger ones is not a crime. And surely, being frugal does not warrant a death sentence. But if the rich man's real problem is not his hard work and frugality, if it is not having made a bad business decision, or that he wants to relax and enjoy life, what is it? "It is," suggests the German theologian, Eduard Schweizer, "functional atheism" – the belief that nothing is happening unless I am making it happen." As Schweizer notes, "Even though we may pay lip service to God, our actions often assume God doesn't exist or is in a coma." We may put, "In God we trust," on our coins, but we more likely trust our protection to the latest security system and the most advanced missile defense shield. We may assume God's sovereignty, yet we hesitate to fully put our trust in One who often seems so distant.

Worry about having enough and our desire for more are ultimately related to how we see ourselves. The rich man sees himself, not God, as the one in charge. In his eyes, he is the owner and therefore assumes his actions are really what control his destiny. But if he had seen himself, not as the owner, but as the steward, he might have viewed things differently. Instead of thinking of himself as a permanent resident whose possessions were his to keep, he might rather have seen himself as a sojourner, a passing traveler, whose land was his to use, but not to possess; something to manage as a loan, but not something to keep or build his future upon. Then, perhaps, his success would not have blinded him to the transitory nature of life and his dependence upon God.

A religious pilgrim, visiting a saint's home, sees only a table, a chair and a bed. Curious, he asks, "Why so little furniture?" "It's all I need," the saint replies, and then asks, "Why do you carry so little with you?" "Well," the pilgrim explains, "I'm only a visitor." The saint, pauses a moment and says, "So am I."

Not only does the rich man see himself as the one in charge, but he sees everything in terms of himself; in his eyes, things exist for his benefit alone. But just as library books have a due date when they are to be returned, so too does our life and all we own. If we remember things are not ours to possess, but to use, we may be less likely to see them as something that adds to our worth. As long as our worth is dependent upon something outside of us, we will forever feel we lack something and don't have enough.

Anthony de Mello, the Indian mystic, tells about a husband who says to his wife, "I'm going to work hard, and someday we'll be rich." The wife, however, sees things differently and responds, "We are already rich, dear, for we have each other; someday maybe we'll have money." Winning the battle with greed has much to do with being content with what we already have – only then can we become unconditionally joyful. As long as our joy depends upon conditions, we are forever conditionally joyful and always feeling we need something that is only to be found when the conditions are "right".

In the end, perhaps more than anything else, having enough depends upon realizing there is only one thing that will satisfy our desire for more; only one thing that will make us absolutely independent of everything else. If we are wise, we will see we are not only rich in things, but rich in our relationship with the One in whose hands our life, and all life, revolves. Choosing God is the one thing that can truly make us independent of everything else, and then, and only then, will we no longer have to worry about having enough.

"Does Prayer Change Anything?"

It was the fall of 1942. Young men were being sent to Europe to fight against Hitler's Germany. The young couple had just gotten engaged when her fiancée received word he was being sent overseas. "I'll pray for you every day," she told him, and so she did. Three months later when word came that Jack had been killed, she told her mother, "When Jack went to war, I prayed every night for his safety, but he was killed. I shall never pray again."

Her response is understandable and perhaps not that uncommon. It suggests that if our prayers are not answered, why should we even bother to pray. If prayer cannot change anything, is there really any use in praying?

While atheists may see prayer as a waste of time and agnostics may doubt the usefulness of prayer, for many religious people there is a great temptation to rush to the defense of God, and say prayer always works even though the outcome may not always be as we desire. But not only are our prayers not always answered as we might wish, in terms of our growth and development as people, we may sometimes be better served when our prayers are not answered. After all, not everything we ask for is good for us.

Most any child would like to stay up late and eat only candy, but parents know a child's welfare is better served by a good night's sleep and a balanced diet. And as adults, our understanding of what we want and what is good for us may not always be that much better. What we want and what God wants for us are not always the same, especially when there's a difference between what we want and what is good for us. When we only pray in order to get what we want, we really do not address ourselves to God, but only to the things we desire or fear, and God becomes only a means to an end – the one who can provide what we need.

If what we expect from prayer is to have our fears removed and our desires satisfied, then we assume that God is behind the counter simply to serve us. When this happens, God becomes a mere means to an end, summoned by a magical incantation, and our prayers are limited to times of fear or special need. We then become like the child who when asked why he prayed at night, but not during the day, replied, "I'm not scared in the morning."

The outcome of our prayers depends not only upon what we ask for, but also upon the kind of god to whom we pray. Is God merely a celestial bellhop granting whatever we desire or is God more concerned about the kind of people we become? In war there are no doubt wives and mothers on both sides praying for the safe return of their husbands and sons.

What kind of God can possibly answer all of their prayers? If God does not manipulate things just to please us, perhaps it is because God is more concerned with our growth and development than with us always getting our way. While it is natural to pray for the safe return of our loved ones, praying and working for peace may be even more important.

Jesus never says that the one who asks God for bread shall receive bread in all circumstances; he rather says that under no circumstances shall he receive a stone. But what does this mean? For starters, it means that even though we may or may not get what we ask for, prayer does change things. One of the first things prayer changes is us. As one of Dostoevski's characters says, "Every time we pray, if our prayer is sincere, there will be new feelings and new understandings that will give us fresh courage." Increasingly, prayer that opens us up to God can make us less self-centered. Helmut Thielicke, the twentieth-century, German theologian notes, "The benefit of prayer is not some miracle it allows, but that our hearts are moved." Perhaps the shift from immature to mature prayer takes place when we increasingly desire what God wants, rather than demand what we want. Where this happens, our life is undoubtedly better even though our circumstances may remain unchanged. The focus of truly mature prayer will surely be as Jesus prayed in the Garden of Gethsemane, "Not my will, but thine be done."

When this shift from ourselves to God occurs, prayer changes not only ourselves, but our relationship with others. As we think about others in a more sympathetic way, we become more ready to be of help to those for whom we pray. Praying for the sick or someone recovering from surgery may lead us to send a get-well card, or visit them, and perhaps even bring a meal. Praying for the homeless or hungry may lead us to a social service involvement where we contribute our gifts for their benefit. Praying for someone who has offended us can lead us to wrestle with forgiveness.

Whatever we present to God as important in our prayers cannot be a matter of indifference to the rest of our living. If we ask God to care about it, we must care about it ourselves. If we struggle in prayer over someone with whom we have experienced difficulty, prayer can increase our power to forgive them and accept someone else's forgiveness. It was Henry Ward Beecher who said in one of his sermons, "I pray on the principle that the wine knocks the cork out of the bottle – where there is an inward fermentation, there must be an outward release."

Ultimately, prayer can change not only us, but our relationship to God. The more we turn to God in prayer, the more God takes on a specific identity. God is no longer just an abstract, ethereal being, but that One who is always available, ready to listen, attentive to our struggles, hurting when we hurt, eager to comfort, and always wanting to call forth our best. God ceases to run errands for us, and instead becomes a friend and confidante with whom we share our hopes and joys, our failures and triumphs.

A fellow clergy recently shared with me that the other night when his four year old daughter finished her evening prayers, he noticed she remained at her bedside for quite some time. When he became impatient and told her to get into bed, she told him, "I was just waiting to see if God had anything to say to me." She is already aware that prayer is not just giving God a list of our concerns, but listening to hear what concerns God may have for us. No wonder Jesus says, "Unless you become like a little child, you shall never enter into the kingdom of heaven."

Prayer may not always bring us miracles, but if it changes our hearts and moves us to act on someone else's behalf that may be miracle enough. Miracle enough because where this happens, our lives are always better, even though our circumstances may remain unchanged. In the end, effective prayer is not measured by how much we manage to get out of God, but by how much of God we manage to get into our daily living. Prayer that truly makes a difference is an act by which we become more God-conscious. Such prayer involves unburdening ourselves – expressing our thanks, our wrongs, our longings, and opening ourselves to God, waiting for God's love to transform us.

Perhaps, the most important question we can ask is not, "Does prayer change anything?" but rather, "Does prayer change me?" What might happen if we would pray, "O God, here I am; use me this day to make a difference in your world."

"What Does It Mean To Follow Jesus?"

He sees a man sitting at the tax office, and says, "Follow me," and the man follows him, and it's as simple as that - or is it? We're tempted to explain Matthew's response in terms of Jesus' charisma. But maybe it would be better to recall that for Matthew the person of Jesus is at least as problematic as for us, and probably more so.

As a tax collector, Matthew is extremely well off financially, knowing he can collect whatever he asks and confident he has the backing of Rome to do so. He is perfectly content with his current position in life. Then one day, an itinerant preacher walks in and says, "Follow me." There's a certain attraction in his bearing, but why should he or anyone else give up a lucrative racket for a gigantic question mark?

All the voice says is, "Follow me." There is no forewarning; no explanation; no attempt to persuade. No cost is mentioned, and no reward is offered. No biographical information is given, but surely there are questions. Who are you? Where are we going? How far? Why should I go? What can I take along? What will it cost? What will be my reward?

Who is this one who asks us to follow? No one seems to be sure – to the people of his day he is an enigma who calls forth a wide range of opinions. To Peter, he is Christ, the son of God. To Judas, he is a commodity worth a mere thirty pieces of silver. To Bartimaeus, he is a healer who cures his blindness, but to the Pharisees, he is a law breaker who is demon possessed and leading people astray.

And to us who contemplate his meaning today, is he anything more? Is he merely a good story teller who gives us a different picture of the world, or is he simply a good man whose example is worth following? Is he a healer and miracle worker who can take away our pain and fulfill our dreams, and be, as some claim, Lord and Savior, or is he outdated and no longer relevant for today's world?

However we may view him, "He comes," in the words of Albert Schweitzer, "as one unknown, without a name, as by the sea so long ago, he came to those who knew him not. He calls to us the same words he spoke to them. Follow me. And he sets to us the tasks that he would have us fulfill in our time. He commands. And to those who obey, whether they be wise or simple, he will reveal himself in the conflicts and tensions and sufferings that we will pass through with him."

Where will we go? Like Abraham we travel to an unknown land. Who knows where? It may be Jerusalem, citadel of the establishment; or it may be more out of the way – like Ephesus or Corinth or Green Lake. It may not be where we want to go, but where we are wanted. Not all places Christ takes his disciples are comfortable, but need, not comfort, is where Christ leads them.

Some of you may be a little uneasy with the appointment of Willy Jackson to be your new pastor. Beginning this July, he will be the first African-American to serve as the minister of this congregation. Some of you may have your doubts about working with a black preacher, yet this is exactly where Christ calls us to grow as his body in Seattle. Working with Willie we may discover God calls us to see our ministry and worth are not found in our skin tones – a discovery long overdue, regardless of our level of comfort.

What can we take along? Maybe the first thing we should recognize is the knowledge of our own unendingly ambiguous motives. Yes, we follow Christ out of love, but also we follow merely out of habit or to be well thought of or because we like the people who belong to the church. Our motives are never pure and seldom clear. But along with this mixture of motives, and more important, we bring with us our knowledge that Christ accepts us wherever we are. The voice that calls us never says, "First, be sure your motives are pure and selfless, and then come and follow." If it did, who of us could follow?

What will be required? Humility that reminds us the pupil is not above his master. Jesus says we who are called to be a light to the world should not make a show of our religion; our left hand is not to know what our right hand is doing and when we pray, we are to do so in private. We are called to be servants; to follow, not lead. This does not, however, mean we lose our raw spirit, enthusiasm, and spontaneity. Our individuality remains, so long as it is in the service of the one we follow.

What is not required is a particular set of moral standards or adherence to a given life style; no single life style can be called Christian. Some have tomato juice before dinner, some have a cocktail; some have scotch and water before going to bed while others gorge themselves on ice cream and cake and some go to bed having eaten nothing. Some protest and march and picket; others quietly work with their families and neighborhood. Only one thing is the same for all – God's love and call to love others.

How far will we be asked to go? As far as we can. Perhaps, like the rich man there will be a point beyond which we cannot go. Perhaps, there will be something we are asked to give up which we prefer to hold on to – to keep tightly in our grasp. But if we are serious, there will be tears – tears not only for the one we follow who is crucified, but tears also for our own lack of courage, our shame, and our regret.

What is our goal? Simply, to seek first the kingdom of God. It is a kingdom without boundaries where no passport is required. No degree or diploma or letter of sponsorship is necessary. All are invited, though to gain access we must forget the morality of the world – the law of competition doesn't play well when the first shall be last. Here, might does not make right and forgiveness replaces revenge; the exalted are humbled, and the humble are exalted. Life in its fullest dimension is found not by acquisition of something more, but by sharing what we have.

Seeking God's kingdom is not a matter of isolated acts of self-denial; it is not just a series of sacrifices or obeying a set of external commands, but only being aware of the one whom we follow. The focus for those who follow is not on the road that is too hard for us, but seeing instead the One who goes before us.

Who, then, is this One we follow? He is the one we begin to know fully only by following. As Frederick Buechner points out, "As we follow, we become, such as we are, his church and his body – a weak thing in most ways, half-hearted, and of little faith, but full of hope for all that." We are, after all, the only body that Christ has in this world; the only hands and feet to do his work. Yet, such is his power that even through us others may be led to follow.

Throughout history people have listened to the teachings of Christ and heard his summons to follow. Some have responded with admiration; some have turned a deaf ear. Each one of us has no doubt at times been in both camps; sometimes singing Christ's praises, and at other times turning a deaf ear. We are not always his eager followers, but of one thing we can be sure – his call to follow will always be there, asking us to take up his yoke and discover - not only is the burden light, it is the doorway to the fulfillment of our deepest longings.

"Why Do Bad Things Happen To Good People?"

One of the great mysteries of human life is the suffering of innocent people. Why a good God allows bad things to happen to good and innocent people is a question that has troubled theologians and philosophers throughout history. While some things may forever remain a mystery, those who suffer the loss of a loved one still cry out for some kind of answer.

This season of Lent is an appropriate time to ask this question since it is a time when we contemplate what it means to follow the way of Jesus, the one who fed the hungry, cured the sick, welcomed the outcast, and forgave sinners, yet ended up hanging from a cross. If there is any answer to innocent suffering, perhaps we shall find it in the suffering and death of this one we call Christ.

When we ask why Jesus was crucified, several things are worth noting. While they may not totally explain why bad things happen to good people, they can provide some helpful clues. One of the most obvious, yet often overlooked, is simply because he was human – a fact that applies to all who suffer without just cause.

Sometimes people, especially those of a religious bent, see Jesus as something of a superman. When he is reported to walk on water, restore sight to the blind, feed thousands with two loaves of bread and five fish, raise the dead, and overcome death, it is easy to see how this elevated status might occur. But regardless of how we may interpret the miracle stories and resurrection accounts, it is a fundamental claim of traditional Christianity that Christ was first of all a human being like you and me. And because Jesus was human, his body was flesh and blood like ours with the same capacity for fatigue, pain, suffering, and death that is the lot of all humans.

While being human does not in itself explain innocent suffering, it does mean we humans are all vulnerable. Morality has nothing to do with human suffering. As the gospel of Matthew points out, "God gives sun and sends rain on the upright and the wicked alike." Jesus explains to those who question why the man in the ninth chapter of John's gospel is born blind, "His blindness is not because he or his parents sinned." It happened, not as a form of punishment, but simply is the outcome of his birth. Bad things can happen to anyone at any time; they are non-discriminatory and quite simply a part of our human lot.

But while innocent suffering may not be a result of anything we do or fail to do, it may be the result of what someone else does or fails to do. As parents, we may suffer because our child commits a crime with which we had nothing to do. But a child may also innocently suffer because of a parent's alcoholism or drug addiction. We may die or be permanently disabled because someone drives while intoxicated or fails to stop at a traffic light. We may suffer because a doctor makes a wrong diagnosis or a druggist fails to inform us of a prescribed drug's harmful side-effects. These mistakes may be made, not out of malice, but even with good intentions. Those responsible may not even be aware of the harmful consequences their actions cause.

Jesus went to the cross partly because certain people willed it to happen as with the priests and mob who shouted, "Crucify him." Other people helped put Jesus there with what they considered a legitimate cause - in Pilate's case, to preserve the peace of Rome; in the case of the soldiers, by simply obeying orders and doing their duty. Judas, by some accounts, betrayed Jesus because he wanted to force Jesus to declare himself the Messiah. In all these cases, Jesus was simply the victim of their humanity or, some might say, their lack of humanity.

With all of us, things may happen that we cannot explain, and their "why" will forever remain a mystery. In these instances, the only meaning to be found may be in our response. The response of Jesus provides a good example of how our response may bring something positive and redemptive out of what appears senseless. Jesus was not a passive victim of the cross; he went there knowing he could have stayed away from Jerusalem or simply toned down his teachings and made peace with the establishment. Yet, he accepted the cross and by his words from it – words of concern for his mother and friend, John, asking them to take care of each other; words of forgiveness for those who had put him there; and words of trust, "Into your hands I commit my spirit," releasing himself into God's hands – used his own suffering to try to bring peace and healing to others. Thus, Jesus makes the cross redemptive, turning something bad into something good and bringing, at least for some, not only wisdom and comfort out of its foolishness and suffering, but ultimately, hope that new life might arise out of death.

When bad things happen to those we love, perhaps we too can bring something redemptive by our response. When a friend is killed in an auto accident, if our own driving and efforts to improve road safety can help prevent future suffering, something good may come out of it. When a tornado strikes a neighboring community, if we join others in providing relief to the survivors and help rebuild what has been destroyed, some hope and healing may help restore what has been lost. If we are reminded how truly precious, yet fragile human life is, and as a result renew our efforts to live each day well, something good may yet come out of tragedy.

It is all right to be angry and rail at those we may hold responsible, including God, so long as we do not let the anger and bitterness either consume us or become destructive. While we may condemn the person responsible for our own or another's misfortune, who of us would want to walk in their shoes? In our hurt and anger, let us pray that not only justice, but also mercy, may be carried out – justice to try to compensate for the loss suffered; mercy to help bring healing even to those responsible.

Why a good God allows bad things to happen has been a conundrum for philosophers and theologians throughout history. Perhaps, the key word is "allows" for God does not treat us as puppets, directing and protecting our every move. Nor does God change the laws of the universe to our benefit. We are given life and the freedom to live it as we choose, but if vehicles are driven at excessive speeds, there is no guarantee that either the driver will be able to maintain control nor that innocent people will be spared suffering. But while God may allow such suffering, God never wills it.

We can feel cheated and cry out against life's unfairness, for like the Psalmist, we know life is not always fair and we don't always get what we want or deserve. We can condemn those we feel responsible and blame God for allowing bad things to happen, but in the end, if we are to find the peace we long for, it may more likely be found remembering, not what we have lost, but what we have been given by the one whom we grieve – someone we have loved, who has given us days of joy and laughter and a deep, abiding, unforgettable memory that will always be sacred. Then, when we are able, we may be able to respond to the sense of loss and hurt in a way that can bring something good from it – something that, like Jesus' example, will help overcome the bad with something good.

"Stories To Live By"

"The destiny of the world is determined less by the battles that are lost and won than by the stories it loves and believes in." C. Simkinson

Some of my fondest Sunday School memories are the Biblical stories that my Sunday School teacher, Mr. Crawford, used to tell. While David and Goliath and Daniel in the lion's den were fascinating stories at the time, later in life, as I came to see the complexity and vulnerability in the lives of many of these Old Testament heroes and heroines of faith, I realized that they were not without their blemishes. Like me, they had feet of clay that revealed their human weaknesses as well as their strengths, and thus became even more real and appealing. They were no longer supermen and women, but people whose lives did not always reflect the glory of God.

Jacob, Jonah, Job, and Moses are four of these giants of the Old Testament whose lives reveal both their shortcomings and their journeys of faith. Each one wrestles with God as they reflect on where life has brought them – sometimes, as in the case of Jacob and Jonah, being forced to come to terms with their less than faithful lives; and sometimes, as in the case of Job and Moses, questioning life's fairness.

Jacob, who has cheated his brother, Esau, out of both his birthright and his father's blessing, is finally, after being on the lam for more than twenty years, preparing to face his brother once more. The night before their meeting, Jacob wrestles with an angel, determined to receive the angel's blessing. It is in many ways the biggest battle of Jacob's life for it is the battle with himself – the one in which he looks at himself in the mirror to decide who he wants to be - not only as a brother to Esau, but also as a person of faith. What can this story tell us about engaging our own divine angels?

Jonah is for many of us, perhaps remembered best as the man swallowed by a whale. But Jonah's real story involves his reluctance to carry out God's condemnation of the city of Ninevah – a reluctance based on his fear that instead of punishing the hated Ninevites, God will take pity on them if they repent of their sins. When Jonah's worst fears come to pass, he sulks and complains that God has not only gone back on his word, but made Jonah look like a fool for proclaiming the city's destruction. When we feel God has disappointed us, how does our response compare to Jonah's?

As Archibald McLeish points out, there is always someone playing Job – people who suffer for no apparent reason. And like Job, there are always people who want to bring us comfort. But however well-intentioned they may be, their attempts to comfort often only deepen our despair. Job's response is one that challenges all of us when our faithfulness to God is not rewarded for it raises the question, "What is our faithfulness based upon?" Does it depend upon receiving some kind of reward, or is it based on something more enduring?

And finally, the story of Moses is another account of someone dealing with what seems like a lack of fairness. Moses' place of prominence in the history of Israel is beyond dispute. He, not only led the Israelites out of Egypt after 430 years of slavery, he also established the Ten Commandments as the legal code that serves as the basis of Jewish law. Yet, he was not permitted to enter the "promised land" himself. His story and the way he handles this disappointment is well worth pondering when we encounter situations in our own life where our dreams are not realized.

"Jacob: Alone in the Night"

It is dark. The animals are bedded down and the campfire is extinguished. Silence hangs over the plain, broken only by the lapping of the stream against its banks. Alone in the night stands Jacob, pondering his life.

Worried about tomorrow, Jacob has sent his family and servants on ahead that he might be alone. He knows his life is about to change, but isn't sure how. Tomorrow he will meet his brother, Esau, whom he hasn't seen in twenty years – not since the day he deceived his father and tricked him into bestowing the blessing intended for his brother, Esau, on himself.

It was Esau's threat to kill him that drove him from home. But that was a long time ago and much has happened since. There was that dream on the way to Harran, assuring him of God's blessing. But who can trust a dream? And there were those fourteen years working for his uncle Laban to gain permission to marry his daughter, Rachel - seven more than he and uncle Laban had originally agreed upon. That seemed a high price to pay for a blessing. Nonetheless, he has managed to accumulate an abundance of family and wealth - eleven sons and a daughter, hundreds of sheep, goats, and cattle, and more servants than he can count.

Jacob is now ready to return home, but what will tomorrow bring? Will Esau take his revenge or will he accept Jacob's peace offering and be reconciled? Playing it safe, Jacob has divided his camp in two, thinking if Esau attacks and destroys one, the other may escape. In addition, he has sent several of his servants ahead to offer Esau gifts – gifts of some two-hundred and twenty goats, another two-hundred and twenty ewes and rams, thirty camels, forty cows, ten bulls, and thirty donkeys. All this, just in the hopes of winning his brother's favor. But will this be enough to win Esau's favor and forgiveness, or will Esau still bear a grudge and seek his life?

Jacob is afraid. He has been fortunate all his life, but how much longer will God's favor rest upon him? Tomorrow will be a time of accounting! Now alone by the stream, Jacob sits and ponders his life. "*It's true, I did obtain Esau's birthright. But was it my fault Esau placed a higher value on satisfying his hunger than holding on to his rights as the first-born? Could I help it that Esau cared so little for the future that he was willing to barter away his privileged position as head of the family?*

And yes, it's true I obtained Dad's blessing in a less than straightforward manner – it was deceitful to take advantage of father's blindness by disguising myself in Esau's clothes, but I was only doing what mother suggested. After all, it was her idea. She was the one who prepared the venison and gave me Esau's clothes to wear.

And yes, I did selectively breed Uncle Laban's flocks in order to build up my own. But look how Laban deceived me – making me work another seven years before I could marry Rachel. Surely, I did no more than even the score."

Thus, Jacob spends the night, reflecting on his past. He knows his life is not perfect, but he has always worked hard and taken advantage of the opportunities that have come his way. Being his mother's favorite has helped, but it's his own hard work that has given him most of what he has; he, not his mother, is responsible for his success.

But in recalling his achievements, can Jacob so easily rationalize all that his life has been? Is he not glossing over his life's shadows? And so, once again Jacob ponders his life. *"But perhaps I've accepted what I've done too quickly? Maybe I've lived with duplicity so long I can no longer call things by their rightful name. When I gained Esau's birthright – was I merely being opportunistic or was it bribery? When I obtained my father's blessing – was I just being clever or was it deceit? And when I selectively bred Laban's flocks was it really just a matter of justice or was it revenge?*

Perhaps, I have confused the true meaning of greatness. I know grandpa Abraham did many great things and is remembered for going into the wilderness and even being willing to sacrifice his only son, Isaac, to prove his faithfulness to God. But the ventures I've made into the wilderness have not brought me honor; all my trips into the wilderness have been to escape someone's wrath. And whenever I've been confronted with the anger of those I've deceived, I've chosen to run away. Am I going to spend all my life running?"

Thus, Jacob spends the night wrestling with his conscience. Faced with the crisis meeting Esau presents, Jacob, troubled and alone, reviews his past. Will he choose to go on running, deceiving and placating? Or will he take hold of himself; stop playing games and pretending?

Scripture says an adversary wrestled with him until the break of day. Only then does the adversary speak, saying, "Day is breaking. Let me go." But Jacob refuses, "I will not let you go until you bless me."

Who can say whether the blessing Jacob receives is what he expects. All that is known is that at dawn Jacob is a different man. No longer is he content to be the son of Isaac and grandson of Abraham. He now has a name all his own –"Israel", for in the words of scripture, "You have shown your strength against God and man and prevailed."

Jacob has fought the biggest battle of his life – the battle with himself. It wasn't a new battle for it has been fought since the first man and woman asked themselves what they had done with their life. It was the battle Christ fought in the Garden of Gethsemane the night before the crucifixion. It is the same battle you and I fight when we look into the window of our life and see our reflection.

When Jacob crosses the river in the morning, he seems calmer than he had been the day before. He still might fight, and even kill and die. But he is no longer alone. Knowing he can no longer ignore his past sins, he is now ready to face whatever the day may bring. As Frederick Buechner has commented, "He has suffered the magnificent defeat of the human soul at the hands of God." And yes, God is the adversary because it is ultimately God with whom we do battle. But this is a beloved enemy because God more than compensates us for what he demands we give up for in giving up, not only every deceit and illusion, but our hearts and treasures as well, we are given our life back.

Like Jacob, we too have our accomplishments and our deceptions; we too have those shadows that we would prefer others not see. We may not have Jacob's wealth and servants and we may not have cheated a brother out of the family inheritance, but who of us can ponder our own life without acknowledging our shortcomings? Like Jacob, we too may one day encounter that dark night of the soul. Like Jacob, when that time comes, we too will be asked to wrestle with the angel if we are to receive God's blessing. It is ours for the taking: but only if we engage the angel. The choice is always ours. Will we run and placate, or will we engage the one battle that is truly worth fighting?

"Jonah: When God Does Not Play By Our Rules"

His name is Jonah. Born in Gath-Hepher during the reign of Jereboam II in 786 B.C., nearly eight centuries before Christ, he is a prophet like his father, Amittai. His greatest desire in life is to please God and keep his commandments. The causes and concerns of God are his concerns as well - to honor and uphold the good; to confront and destroy evil.

In Jonah's eyes, the greatest evil of his day is found in Nineveh, a city of over one million inhabitants on the east bank of the Tigris River. It is the capital of the Assyrian empire and known for the grandeur of its palatial buildings and the massive walls that surround them – walls more than two hundred feet high, and wide enough that two chariots can ride side-by-side on top of them.

Nineveh itself is filled with greed, treachery, and deceit. Sacking Palestine seems to be its number one sport. The Ninevites have overrun Palestine countless times, looting its possessions, burning its homes, raping its women, killing the children, and even having the gall to decorate the walls of their public buildings with the children's skins.

To better understand Jonah's feelings toward Nineveh and what God has asked him to do, let us listen to him explain it in his own words: *Given my hatred of the Ninevites, I suppose it's hard for you to understand my response to God when he asks me to go to Nineveh and denounce it. It certainly isn't that Nineveh doesn't deserve to be denounced nor am I afraid of what they might do to me. What worries me is God. What if I denounce the city as God has asked me, and they repent of their sins? Will God change his mind about destroying them? What if God has a change of heart and decides not to destroy them? If God changes his mind, forgives them their sins, and excuses their guilt, think how it will make me look. Why, I'll look like a fool! Who will ever take what I say seriously again? And I can't say that I would blame anyone either.*

So when God calls Jonah to go east to Nineveh, Jonah goes west to Joppa. His explanation is simple: *I think I need time to think things over. I've been doing whatever God's asks all my life; I've hardly had a moment to call my own. I need a vacation; someone else can go to Nineveh.*

Jonah decides to spend his vacation in Spain, and books passage at Joppa for Tarshish, the most distant port to which ships are bound. On the way, however, the ship runs into a terrible storm. The boat is being tossed from side to side. Fearing for their lives and afraid the ship might actually sink, the sailors begin throwing the cargo overboard, hoping to lighten the ship and keep it from going down.

In the midst of this frantic activity, the ship's captain finds Jonah asleep in the hold below, awakens him and demands, "*Call on your God...perhaps he will spare us and not leave us to die.*" But before Jonah can do anything, the sailors decide to draw lots to see who is responsible for bringing this bad luck. So they cast lots, and when the lot points to Jonah, they begin questioning him, "*Tell us*," they ask, "*what is your business*? *Where do you come from*? *What is your country and nationality*?"

Jonah replies, "*I am a God-fearing Hebrew, and I'm afraid this storm is because of me for I have run away from the Lord. Throw me overboard, and you'll be saved.*" The sailors are seized with terror at this, and not wanting to be responsible for an innocent man's death, row all the harder trying to bring the boat to shore, but to no avail.

Finally, fearing for their own safety and praying that they will not be held responsible for an innocent man's death, they throw Jonah overboard. Almost at once, he disappears into the sea, and it stops raging. At this the sailors are filled with dread, and fearing God's displeasure, vow to never displease him again.

According to scripture, a whale swallows Jonah, and he remains in its belly for three days and three nights. From the belly of the whale, Jonah prays to God for deliverance, and promises he will be his faithful servant from now on. Then, a miracle happens and the whale vomits Jonah onto dry ground.

As he recovers his bearings, Jonah is not certain where he is or exactly what has happened, but one thing is clear – God is not through with him. Once again he hears God's call to go to Nineveh and preach to the people what God tells him. *Alright, Lord, I see that you mean business. If we're going to show people they reap what they sow, then Nineveh must pay for its wickedness.*

Catching another boat, Jonah makes his way back to the city where God has called him. Once there, he marches to the king's palace, and there proclaims in a loud voice, "Nineveh, listen to me. In forty days you will be overthrown." Eager for the city's destruction, Jonah prays that he will not be disappointed.

When the king hears Jonah's pronouncement, he puts on sackcloth, covers himself with ashes, and orders a public fast, appealing to his fellow Ninevites to abandon their wicked ways. But Jonah is not to be duped. In his eyes, the king's actions are not surprising; they are simply a ploy to change God's mind. Jonah tells the king, "God will not be taken in by your phony repentance. Do you think God's mercy can so easily be manipulated? You can't turn God's mercy on and off like a spigot."

But when God sees the Ninevites repent, he does indeed change his mind, and instead of destroying the city, he forgives the people for their sins. Jonah is livid with anger. *I should have known better than to think the Ninevites would get what they deserve. What a fool I've been!* Then, his rage turns into pouting and self-pity. *What am I? Just a plaything to be ridiculed? I've been faithful to you all these years, while these Ninevites have been going about their wicked ways, enjoying themselves. Now look what's happened. This makes me look like a blooming idiot. Aren't my faithfulness and obedience worth anything?*

Exhausted and depressed, Jonah goes to the edge of the city where he sits on a hill and licks his wounds. The sun is beating down on him, but as he sits there, a castor oil plant grows up to provide him shade. The next day, however, a worm attacks the plant and it dies, leaving Jonah without the protection from the sun it has afforded him. At this point, feeling totally defeated, Jonah moans, "*I might as well be dead as to go on living.*"

Questioning Jonah's anger and petulance, God asks, "If you are concerned for the castor plant, which grew and perished in a night, why should I not be concerned for the people of Nineveh? Jonah has no answer.

Like Jonah, do we sometimes feel God has let us down, rewarding our enemies and ignoring our faithfulness? If so, perhaps we need to remember God does not always play by our rules. Our love for some and hatred of others is not shared by God, for God's love and mercy are universal. Of all God's gifts, mercy is usually the one we need most. Yet, it is often the one we find most difficult to grant others. We are eager to receive it, but not so eager to pass it on. Thankfully, God's mercy is bigger than ours!

"Job: Troubled Innocence"

There once lived a man named Job. He was the embodiment of virtue. Unlike his famous ancestors, Jacob and Jonah, he had never deceived anyone nor disobeyed God. He was honest and forthright in all his dealings; indeed, his integrity was unquestioned. He feared God and honored him with a life that upheld justice and avoided evil. There wasn't a person in need that he didn't try to help.

But why shouldn't he have been a good man? Look what he has - a faithful and loving wife, seven capable sons and three beautiful daughters, seven thousand sheep, three thousand camels, five hundred oxen, a like number of donkeys, and a household full of servants. Wealth, family, influence, and reputation – they are all his.

Noting this, Satan challenges God, saying "It's easy to be God-fearing when you're so richly blessed. Why wouldn't Job be pious in exchange for such privileges? But what if all these benefits were taken away? Will Job then remain faithful, or will he curse you to your face?"

God is confident his servant Job will remain steadfast in his faith, and so he gives the devil permission to do with Job whatever he likes so long as, "You keep your hands off his person." The devil agrees and soon after disaster strikes Job.

One after the other, he loses his livestock, his fortune, his home, and his children. Messenger follows messenger, with one arriving as the other is still making his report on the latest loss. "The Sabaeans attacked and carried off your oxen; the Chaldaens raided the camels, a fire destroyed the sheep; a tornado swept across the desert and destroyed your eldest son's home, while he was entertaining your other children, and they are all dead."

Job is in shock. He tears his clothes, shaves his head, and goes into mourning. To add to his misery, his body breaks out in a rash, and his skin is covered with sores and blisters. But despite his loss and pain, Job's faith remains unshaken. His only words are, "Naked I came from my mother's womb and naked I shall return. Yahweh gave; Yahweh has taken back. Blessed be the name of Yahweh!" In all his misfortune, Job, at least at first, neither commits any sin, nor reproaches God.

Later, however, he begins to lament his fate and asks God for an explanation as to why such misery has befallen him. "My life would have been better had I never been born. Why was I not still-born? Why has this happened to me? What have I done to deserve such fate? God, I have never violated any of your laws or transgressed any of your commandments – why are you letting this happen to me? Why do you permit the innocent to suffer?"

Archibald MacLeish, the poet who wrote the Broadway play, J.B., says through the play's narrator, "There's always someone playing Job. Millions and millions of mankind burned, crushed, broken, mutilated, slaughtered, and for what? Job is everywhere we go, his children dead, his work for nothing, counting his losses, scraping his boils, questioning everything – the times, the stars, his own soul, God's providence."

And as with Job, there are always people who want to bring us comfort. The first of Job's comforters is Eliphaz. He appeals to Job's piety, and asks, "Does not the integrity of your life give you hope? If I were you," he adds, "I should appeal to God and lay my case before him, for he who wounds is he who soothes, and the hand that hurts is the hand that heals."

Encouraged to make his appeal to God, Job responds, "Show me, God, where I have been at fault, and I shall say no more. Show me where I went wrong that I can correct it. Then, at least, if I am guilty, I can understand some reason for my suffering. Does my desperate speech deserve censure? Look at me, man to man. Suppose I have sinned, what have I done to you? And if I have offended you, can you not overlook my fault? After all, I shall soon be lying in the dust."

At this point, a second "would-be" comforter, Bildad, speaks, "God does not punish without cause. When we suffer, it is to teach us forbearance and patience. Do not reject the discipline of the Almighty. Like ore, we are cast into the furnace that we might emerge fine gold."

Listening to Bildad pontificate, angers Job, and he interrupts, "Save your moral platitudes. Anyway, what gives you the right to speak for God? And if suffering is such a great benefit, why hasn't everyone received the gift? I'll gladly exchange places with you."

Hearing Job's response, a third comforter, Zophar, speaks next, "Can you or anyone claim to fathom the depth of God's wisdom? Reconsider you attitude, stretch out your hands toward God, and you will forget your misery. You are not the only one who suffers. Look around and you'll see there are plenty of others who carry heavy burdens."

"Yes," Job agrees, "I know I'm not the only one who suffers, but how can I find comfort in someone else's misery? My own is more than I can bear. How do you expect me to carry another's?"

What Job gets from his comforters, as well-intentioned as they may be, is a series of absolutely true and beautiful religious clichés and moral platitudes. Instead of bringing comfort, they only deepen his despair. Not only is there no justice; there is no comfort. Job's friends are of no help, and now there is no one but God. Unfortunately, God has refused to speak.

But then, in the midst of his despair, Job hears a voice out of the whirlwind. "Where were you when I laid the foundations of the earth? Who shut in the sea, and made the clouds? Where were you when the morning stars first sang? Will you reproach, God? Answer me."

Chastened, Job answers, "I have heard of thee by the hearing of the ear, but now my eyes see thee. I am undone. In dust and ashes, I repent." All during his suffering, Job has proclaimed his innocence; now, in humility, he suddenly repents. What has happened to Job? Has God over-powered him? Has God beaten him down with his majesty and power, and forced him into submission? Or has Job come to a new understanding of what it means to be faithful to God?

Always before Job has believed his faithfulness will be justly rewarded. Now he begins to see that true faithfulness is not to be determined by what happens to him; it is not based on receiving some kind of reward for good behavior; it is rather, knowing that God is to be loved and honored for God's sake alone. And if this is true, what about us? What is the basis of our faithfulness to God? Do we worship God, hoping for some reward? Does it depend upon what happens to us, what burdens we bear or riches we acquire? Or is our worship of God, for God's sake alone? Can we, like Job, come to worship God simply for who God is – our creator and redeemer?

"Moses: At Journey's End"

What is the view like from Mt. Nebo? As mountains go in Washington, it hardly classifies as one with its 2600 foot altitude. But in terms of the life of the man who freed the Hebrews from Egypt and gave them the Ten Commandments, it provides a view of everything he has lived for. Yet, it is to become the scene of his greatest disappointment.

Standing on the peak of Mt. Nebo, Moses is given a view of Canaan, the land that is modern day Palestine, and more importantly for Moses, the land that God had promised Abraham would be the homeland of the Jewish people. For over six hundred years the Jews have lived with that promise, and now – here at last, its rich, fertile plains and river valleys stretch before them, beckoning their entrance. But in the midst of this beautiful vision, Moses hears the words that are the source of his life's greatest disappointment, "This is the land I swore to Abraham that I would give to his descendants. I have let you see it with your own eyes, but you shall not cross over into it."

One can only imagine how Moses must feel upon hearing these words. Scripture gives little indication how he must have felt. Does he argue with God, pleading his case? Does he bewail the injustice, or does he simply resign himself to the verdict, accepting it as his fate? To see the promised land, and then be told he shall not enter it is a definite slap in the face. It would be like waiting your whole life to take a trip around the world, buying your tickets, and then having your spouse die the day before you leave. Or, on a more mundane level, like waiting all summer to see your favorite baseball player, going to the game, and finding out he has come down with the flu and will not play.

To fully appreciate the impact this news must have had on Moses, it is important to review his life. When we remember where he has come from, what he has had to put up with, and what he has accomplished, it is easy to see why he might choose to ignore this verdict. The internal struggle Moses feels cannot be easily resolved for his is no ordinary life; indeed, it reads like a Hollywood script – from slavery to the royal court, from murderer to fugitive, and from forty years in the wilderness to an encounter with a burning bush that leads to the eventual liberation of his people from slavery. If what he hears on Mt Nebo causes him to reflect on his life, there is plenty of material to review.

Let us imagine for a moment Moses' internal struggle. *After all I've been through, after all I've endured, after what I have done for these Hebrew people, what kind of a reward is this? Just look at what I have had to put up with – a life that began in tears, where my mother hid me in a basket so I would not be slaughtered. And then, after growing up in the royal palace, I risked my fortune, freedom, and future to save the life of a total stranger only to become alienated from the very people whose life I had defended. Forced to become a fugitive, I ended up in Midian, where I married Zipporah, raised two sons, and working with my father-in-law, Jethro, still managed to carve out a rather peaceful, idyllic existence until that encounter with the burning bush.*

Following God's call has not been easy; going back to Egypt meant putting up with Pharoah's stubbornness and wrath, enduring the maggots, flies, frogs, locusts, festering boils, and hail, and making an exhaustive run from his pursuing army. And crossing the Red Sea hardly brought relief. Those forty years in the wilderness were filled with plenty of turmoil too – war with the Amalekites, constant worry about food and water, betrayal by my own brother, almost daily complaints from those I rescued that they were better off living as slaves - no gratitude or even friendship was given. Despite giving up my peaceful existence in Midian and obeying God's call to liberate these ungrateful Hebrews from their slavery, I feel lonely and totally unappreciated.

*But what I've had to put up with is only part of the story; an even bigger part is what I have accomplished. I have led the Jews out of Egypt (*after 430 years of slavery*), overcoming both Pharoah's resistance and the Hebrew people's complacency and complaints. I received the Ten Commandments on Mt. Sinai and established one of the most comprehensive legal codes ever compiled. I built the Tabernacle and Ark, which served as both the stabilizing and sustaining point of reference for our Hebrew worship life as we traveled through the wilderness. I conducted the census and organized the twelve Jewish tribes, both of which were essential for maintaining order and morale. I instituted the office of the priesthood, and set up our liturgical calendar and guidelines for observing purification rites and sacrifices. And more than once I defended these Hebrews against Yahweh's wrath, most notably when they made an idol of the golden calf.*

I list the things I've endured and these accomplishments, not with any regret or to be boastful, but simply to ask, do they not entitle me to at least enter the promised land, even if I must die there. To stand here on Mt. Nebo and view the promised land is nice, but it is no substitute for actually being there.

Whether Moses actually entertained any of these thoughts is, of course, pure conjecture. If he had any ill feelings about being barred from entering the promised land after all he has put up with and all he has accomplished, it is not evident. Instead of voicing any complaints or exhibiting any bitterness, Moses handles the greatest disappointment of his life, not with curses and murmurings against God, but by pronouncing a final blessing upon the Israelites before he dies.

His blessing was surely more than an act of resignation or a magnanimous gesture for it indicates a man who sees life, not only in terms of himself, but in terms of the generations who will follow him. Thus, his blessing is an expression of faith – faith that life goes on, even when our particular contribution ends. It proclaims that others can be trusted to continue to build what we have started, and that the promises of God will be realized, even when darkness surrounds our own life.

The story of Moses is the story of one of the most central figures in Jewish history. His accomplishments speak for themselves. His greatness can be measured in many different ways, but one of the most important, yet often over-looked, is the way he handled what must surely have been one of the greatest disappointments of his life. His response from Mt. Nebo asks each of us how we handle our own disappointments in life. Do we cave in to depression, do we rail against the unfairness of life, or like Moses, can we rise above our disappointment, remembering to bless those who will live after us, and put our trust in the promises of God that the dreams we have only seen from afar may be realized some day in the future through those who come after us?

Part II – Living in Today's World

"Knowing What Counts"

"True wisdom is to know what is worth knowing."
H. Humphrey

What is worth knowing is basically a value question, and how we measure value is always subjective – it depends to a great extent upon how we see ourselves in the world. For some people, money and health are at the top of their list; for others, it is a good job and friends. For Christians, Paul suggests faith, hope, and love.

The four subjects I have chosen to focus on are all "T" words – time, talent, timing, and temptation. Each one of these four plays a significant role in whatever values we uphold and, depending upon how we deal with them, is a crucial determinant in helping shape our character.

Time is the backdrop against which all our thoughts and actions take place. It is the one daily ration everyone receives equally. Using our allotment wisely means finding a balance between work and play, action and reflection, time with others and time alone; it also means knowing when to say "no" as well as "yes". And most important of all, as Luke's parable of the dinner party illustrates, it means distinguishing between what is merely urgent and what is truly important. Ecclesiastes rightly notes, "There is a time and a season for everything," but not everything is in season.

Unlike time, talent is not distributed equally; some of us have an abundance of gifts, while others of us possess only a few. The number of gifts, however, is not nearly as important as the use to which we employ them. If we use well the gifts we have, our lives will be enhanced and our capabilities will grow. The parable of the talents makes it clear that God does not ask us what we have or how it compares with what others may have, but he does ask us what we are doing with what we have. The only gifts we need to grieve are those we bury for they are the only ones God can't use.

Timing is a matter of knowing when to hold on and when to let go. It is a crucial issue that confronts us at every stage of life. It can happen with a job, a marriage, a friendship, a change of residence, or any decision that involves staying or leaving. If we hold on to a past relationship or experience too long, it can make it difficult for us to be open to what the future brings. Even though it is natural and important to grieve what we've lost, if we idolize a past relationship too much and refuse to let it go, we may never allow ourselves to fully enter into a new one.

Temptation is not always just a choice between "right" and "wrong"; often it is a choice between the "good" and the "better". Serving our own interests does not always serve the common good, and as the temptations Jesus faces in the desert point out, serving the common good may not always serve the higher interests to which God calls us. When temptation comes it raises the question of our identity, asking not only whose interests will we serve, but also raising two further questions, "In whom or what do we trust?" and "Do we see ourselves in isolation or in relationship?"

“Using Our Time Wisely?

It seems we are rarely friends with time; when we are in a hurry, or getting our first drivers license or waiting for a plane that’s already late, time moves too slowly. But when we’re enjoying our vacation and wanting time to slow down, it moves too fast. How can we live without feeling time’s weight either pulling us too fast, or holding us back too long?

Efficiency experts will tell us it’s all a matter of time management. According to them, we have plenty of time to do whatever we want; what is at issue is simply how we use our time. When we complain that we don’t have enough time, they will remind us that we have all there is.

The familiar words of Ecclesiastes and Jesus’ parable about the banquet each provide some helpful clues as to how we may best manage our time. The former suggests there is a time and a place for everything, and the later emphasizes that not every moment is of equal worth. The key is knowing the right time and the right response.

If we take seriously the idea that there is a time and a place for everything, several points are worth noting. Three that we may want to pay attention to are: finding the right balance in our life between work and play, quiet time and active time, and time with others and time alone; realizing nothing we experience is without value; and understanding that saying “no” may be as important as saying “yes”.

One problem we can encounter is that we sometimes work so hard we have no energy for play so that when we’re not working all we want to do is collapse in front of the television and munch our favorite snack. And when we start putting on a few extra pounds and our spouse complains because we never do anything fun, we either become defensive and feel guilty or go out and play so hard, we have no energy for work.

Making time for everything requires that we pay careful attention to how we use our energy. Finding some quiet time to read and reflect on our life may give us the kind of perspective needed to find a better balance between our work and our play time, our time alone and our time for socializing. When we have a family, finding time to play with our kids, spend quality time with our spouse, hold down a job, and enjoy friends and a hobby is never easy, but it may be essential in attaining a healthy and balanced life.

One thing that may help us find this balance is learning to say “no”. For people who have a strong sense of responsibility, this is especially important. We need to know that none of us is indispensable, and no one person can "do it all". One simple thing that may help is not answering the phone during dinner, letting the answering service do what it's designed to do. Another is to make sure the cell phone is not a constant companion; there are times to be connected, and times to disconnect so we can do other things like read and pray and play with our children or talk with our spouse.

Another thing to regulate, if not say "no" to, is our obsessions. For some, this means limiting their time answering e-mail or playing games on the computer, for others it may mean restricting their hours spent watching sports. For parents who are answering their child's every beck and call, it may mean giving the children a choice as to what they can do, helping them realize they will not always be able to do everything they want and other people have needs as well.

There's a time for everything also means nothing is without value. Times of strife, suffering, and waiting are as necessary to our maturity as are times of harmony, joy, and engagement. Growing old can teach us patience and appreciation for past experience if we learn to accept it. Interruptions can break our train of thought, but they can also give us new insight; they can put us behind schedule, but they can also put our priorities in perspective, and help us realize not every moment is of equal value.

As the story in Luke's gospel points out – decisive moments do exist. If those invited to the dinner party had seen its importance, they undoubtedly would have put aside their excuses and made it a point to attend. The importance of responding to those situations in life that usher in God's kingdom is at the heart of this story. God does not intend we answer everything with equal speed and at full force, but some cries for help should not go unheeded.

There are some times that demand a total, unqualified response; moments when we must be ready to drop all other matters. Elizabeth Kubler-Ross, the author of Death and Dying, relates just such a time when she was hosting a New Year's Eve party one year. Guests were coming and the hors de-oeuvres were ready in the oven when a call came from the hospital from one of her patients who was dying and asked to see her. She hated to leave her guests and ask her husband to take over, but knew it was more important to be with her dying patient.

Though not so dramatic, I had three occasions this past week that caused me to acknowledge there's a difference between things we think are urgent and things that are truly important. The first happened during a hospital visit. It was the first of four visits I had set up for the afternoon – visits that I wanted to make before picking up my son to take him to the dentist. I was just telling the patient "goodbye", when he said "I'm scared I'm going to die." The look in his eyes told me it was not the time to leave.

The second happened the next morning as I was running out the door to get a good start on the day, and heard Pat say, “I need to talk to you.” The sound in her voice made it clear it wasn’t just a request to pick up something from the store.

Later in the day, the third thing happened when my daughter greeted my return home from work with, “Daddy, will you play with me?” I had felt the need to spend more time with her for some time; I sensed she was growing up, and there was a growing distance between us. But at that moment I had to run to the store to buy groceries and had planned to mow the lawn before dinner.

What is urgent, and what is important? Responding to another’s pain, responding to one’s spouse, and playing with one’s daughter – these are truly important! Keeping to one’s schedule, getting a good start on the day, catching up with household chores – these may be urgent, but they are not important in any ultimate sense.

How can we live without feeling time’s weight? It has to do with finding a time and place for everything and keeping a careful eye on the difference between what is merely urgent and what is truly important. It’s not always easy, but it helps to remember there is one to whom we are ultimately obedient - the One who has given us life and wants us to live it in the fullest sense. Instead of rushing to and fro, trying to meet our deadlines and keep our head above water, worrying about so many things, it may help to remember there’s a dinner party awaiting all those who make no excuses when it comes to answering the calls that truly matter. Let us never forget: there’s a difference between what is urgent and what is truly important!

"Using What We Have"

There's a story told about Michelangelo pushing a huge piece of rock down a street. A curious neighbor sitting lazily on the porch of his house calls to him and inquires why he is laboring so over an old piece of stone. In response, the great sculptor is reported to have answered, "*Because there is an angel in this rock that wants to come out.*"

This story suggests there may be an angel inside each of us, waiting to be released. Our task is to shape and transform the raw materials we each have at our disposal into something beautiful and worthwhile so they become houses, pictures, bridges, or something yet to be discovered. How we do this, how we "build the earth" to use Teilhard de Chardin's phrase, is determined by the use of our gifts - the subject of this morning's very provocative parable of the talents.

If you have a soft spot for underdogs, you probably feel the one-talent servant gets the short end of the stick. Not only does he have less to start with, what he has is taken from him. It doesn't seem fair that the rich get richer and the poor lose even what little they have. And besides, what has he done to be treated so harshly? After all, why should he be punished for simply giving back what he has received? Hasn't he fulfilled his obligation to preserve and return what the master gave him? He did not lose it or make it less valuable. Yes, he is cautious – but is that a sin? And how is he harming the master in giving him what he understands the master wants? Isn't the master just being mean and arbitrary?

But before we condemn the master it may be important to ask if the one-talent servant's image of the master is an accurate one. Is the master the hard-hearted man of the third servant's description, one who reaps what he does not sow? Or is he gracious and generous as the first two servants experience him?

If we look at what the master does with the one talent he takes back, it is clear his response is not determined by a desire for personal gain. He doesn't keep the talent he takes back for himself, but rather gives it away to encourage those who have made good use of what they were given. It isn't his own gain that concerns him, but rather the way the servants use what they have received.

This suggests that the one-talent servant's downfall is two-fold. First, he pre-judges the master, and secondly, he lets fear determine his actions. Knowing the master to be a hard man who reaps where he does not sow, he decides the best thing to do with the talent he has been given is to bury it so he can give it back. But what his judgment fails to realize is that the master is more concerned about seeing his talent put to work than merely having it returned. There is, of course, a time to save and a time to spend, but his downfall is pre-judging what is expected and not being open to see the master is not only demanding; he is also encouraging to those who put their talents to work.

While labels make it easy to divide the world into friends and enemies, they can also foster an attitude that creates fear and misunderstanding. So when the one-talent servant becomes more concerned about protecting what he has than risking its loss, he loses even what he has. If he knew the master reaped where he did not sow, he should have realized that merely giving back what he has been given will not be satisfactory. Fear does not diminish his accountability.

Being cautious and safe is not always to be recommended. Defending the status quo is not helpful when it prevents us from exercising our gifts. Taking risks, of course, means moving out of our comfort zone, but unless we go beyond the familiar we'll never discover all the wild possibilities God intends for us. George Bernard Shaw once told a friend, "You see things as they are and ask, 'why'? I dream things that never were and ask, 'why not'?" Unless we're willing to look beyond the past and move beyond the status quo, we'll never create a new world.

But this parable is not only about the dangers of pre-judging people and letting fear dictate our actions, it also seems to be directed at those who try to make sure of their own rightness before God by understanding "goodness" in a passive sense – one avoids sinning by simply not taking any chance of offending God. Perhaps, this is what Martin Luther understood when he said, "If we sin, let us sin boldly."

To those who keep comparing themselves with someone else comes the word that it is unimportant how many talents anyone has; if we use what we have, our lives will be enhanced and our capacity will grow. One gift is not superior or inferior to another. Christ does not relate this parable to embarrass all one-talent people. He is not suggesting that only those who have will be given more, but rather that only those who <u>use</u> what they have will be given more. What counts most is not the number of talents we possess, but how we use them. While distribution of talents is never equal, we are all called to some responsibility. In God's scheme of things, we all have some part to play. There are no unholy gifts – all gifts come from God, and each one needs to be used if the symphony of God's harmony is to be heard in all its richness. The only gifts we need to grieve are those we bury for those are the only gifts God can't use.

While this parable says nothing about the equality of gifts or the equality of distribution, it does promise the same reward to all – the joy of being a creator. The servant with two talents and the one with five talents both receive the same pronouncement, "Well done, good and trustworthy servant; you have shown you are trustworthy in small things, I will trust you with greater things. Come and join in your master's joy."

To claim a future worth having we must give up this image of the stern master (God) for it is this understanding that freezes the servant in fear, and makes him so timid and reticent. To enter fully into the joy of the master we must act boldly; not with fear, but with confidence. What we are given can then be set free to grow and multiply. Is this not how we discover our God-sized possibilities? When we let go our need to preserve what we have and give up our fear of losing it we discover where our joy is found; found, not in saving the gifts we have, but in giving them away.

In her book, The Eighth Day of Creation, Elizabeth O'Connor claims that when we deny our gifts, we blaspheme against the Holy Spirit for in her view the story of creation is found in every man, woman, and child. As she puts it, "Since the day of our conception, the Spirit has brooded over the formless, dark void of our lives, calling *us* into existence through our gifts until they are fully developed." By creating us in his image God has given us the responsibility of continuing with Him the creation of the world. If we are to take seriously our creation in God's image, then let us join with God in the forward march of his continuing creation. God does not ask us what we have or how it compares with what others may have, but he does ask us what we are doing with what we have. And in the final analysis, is not this what really counts?

"Knowing When to Hold On; When to Let Go"

One of my favorite memories growing up was going to the circus. The clowns were entertaining and the lion tamer brave beyond belief, but the thing I found most fascinating was the high-wire act. Watching the trapeze artists with their split-second timing as they let go of one swing and grabbed hold of another was truly breath-taking, especially when a back-flip or somersault preceded catching the second swing. Without a net below, there was no room for error; the timing was of ultimate importance.

Knowing when to hold on and when to let go is a critical issue that confronts us many times. Early or late, it can come at any stage in life. It can come for a music student or an athlete when progress in his or her playing ability seems to have reached a plateau, and he or she has to decide whether it's worth the effort to continue. It can come for parents when they've spent money on the musical instrument and paid for private lessons only to discover the child is reluctant to practice. It can confront us in marriage when things begin to sour and we start questioning, not only the usefulness of counseling, but even whether it's worth it to continue the relationship. It can happen with a job when advancement seems remote or we get bored and lose interest, but we're not sure we can find something else with better benefits. It happens to many of us older people when taking care of the yard and house become more and more time consuming and exhausting, but we're not yet sure we're ready to move into an apartment or condominium. And it can come to any of us when an organization or club to which we belong no longer holds the same interest or meets the same needs it once did, but we hesitate to drop out for fear we may upset the friends we've made.

Knowing when to hold on and when to let go confronted Jesus as well when he had to decide whether to go to Jerusalem or stay in Galilee. As this morning's text suggests, Jesus' brothers knew that if his ministry was to truly impact the life of Israel, he would need to go to Jerusalem. Galilee was where Jesus had performed most of his ministry, teaching the beatitudes, feeding the multitudes, turning water into wine, and healing the nobleman's son. But Galilee was the backwater part of the country – the rural area. If he was to make an impact that had any political consequence, it had to be done in Jerusalem where the powerful reigned. But to go to Jerusalem was risky. His teaching was threatening because it transcended so much of the Jewish law, and often stood in opposition to the religious leadership. He could, of course, stay in obscure Galilee and live in relative comfort, but should he? Or should he dare to enter Jerusalem and risk confrontation with the most powerful?

In all of these situations, both the ones we face and the one Jesus faced, we are dealing with dreams and expectations – either our own or someone else's. Dreams and expectations play a crucial role in life. They can have either positive or harmful consequences, inspiring our highest achievements or immobilizing us and locking us into places that limit our growth Whether they inspire or tyrannize us is often a matter of timing - knowing when to hold on to these dreams and expectations and when to let them go.

How could Jesus know whether to go to Jerusalem or stay in Galilee? How can we know when to hold on and when to let go? We may ask for divine guidance, but there is no assurance it will be forth coming. There is no manual we can turn to for an answer, but let me suggest three things we may find helpful.

First, let us not search for the absolutely right decision, but rather for the best possible decision in the circumstances we face. In most situations, there is no absolutely right answer. What we might condemn or find unacceptable in one instance, might be the most life-giving in another.

In seminary, one of my ethics professors once presented us with the situation some women faced during World War II. In order to feed their children, these women were asked to exchange sexual favors for food. In theory, we find it easy to condemn any form of prostitution, but if the choice is between feeding our hungry child or keeping our conscience clear, what do we do?

Almost every decision we make involves some compromise, which usually means giving up something we might want to keep for something we desire even more. There are few situations that don't have some good and some bad. Ending a marriage is not something we imagine will ever occur when we stand at the altar, and while it is not recommended as a solution to marriage difficulties, it is sometimes not only a last resort, but in the case of domestic abuse, it may be the best course of action to take. Divorce is sometimes an easy way out that avoids any serious effort to heal what is wrong; but it can also be the right thing to do in order to end an abusive relationship.

A second factor that can help us know when to hold on and when to let go involves being prepared. Decisions have a way of sneaking up on us. How often is a parent prepared for a teenager's pregnancy? How many of us felt really prepared for marriage, or the birth of our first child, or retirement? While no amount of planning can ever make us totally prepared for knowing when to hold on and when to let go, thinking about how we would want to respond in advance of making any decision can be helpful, especially when we try to relate God's point of view to our own. Throughout Jesus' life, the time he spent in prayer was at the heart of his decisiveness. "Not my will, but thine be done," guided his decision in the Garden of Gethsemane and throughout his ministry.

The third thing to keep in mind when deciding when to hold on and when to let go is the realization that God's love is bigger and stronger than any decision we make. For any of us, our relationship with God is ultimately more important than the "rightness" of any particular decision we make. Knowing we are surrounded by God's love in both our "holding on" and in our "letting go", we can relax as we seek to let God's love guide our decision, for in our Creator's hands, even our "wrong" decisions can be transformed.

Knowing when to hold on to his ministry in Galilee and when to let it go and move on to Jerusalem was not an easy decision for Jesus. As John's gospel tells the story, holding on and letting go is a tricky business, even for Jesus. He neither enters Jerusalem when or as his brothers wish. When they urge him to go, he says, "the time is not ripe." And when he does go, he does not make a public entrance as they wish, but rather he enters in secret. It is not always easy to discern the right time to let go of one thing and take hold of the next. But fortunately, for us as for Jesus, our relationship with God is more important than perfection. God's love surrounds us whether we are "holding on" or "letting go", and this unconditional love is more important than any decision we make. So as we struggle to know when to hold on and when to let go, may we seek to let God's love guide us, never forgetting the love of the One whom we seek to embody will always surround and uphold all that we do.

When Temptation Comes

These are undoubtedly two of the most well-known stories of temptation in the Bible – one invites Adam and Eve to eat the fruit of the tree of knowledge; the other asks Jesus to use his divine power to prove he is the son of God. In the desert, Jesus resists the devil's temptation; in the garden, Adam and Eve don't. What can each of these stories teach us about facing our own temptations?

As with Adam and Eve, when temptation comes to us it is often ushered in by seeds of doubt and lack of trust.. The snake sows seeds of doubt when he asks, "Did God really say you are not to eat of any tree in the garden?" And he reinforces this doubt by adding, "God knows you will not die…your eyes will be opened, and you will be like gods."

In this subtle way, the snake encourages Adam and Eve to wonder if God is withholding something from them. Do we not ask with them, "How does God know what's best for me?" After all, is not the desire for wisdom a legitimate desire? And too, what right does God have to thwart such a noble desire? If God has given us dominion over all the earth, why not eat from this tree? Why not explore the unknown?

Similarly, the devil tempts Christ in the desert when he prefaces his first two temptations with the words, "If you are the son of God," If you are the son of God, why shouldn't you use your divine power to turn stones into bread and feed the hungry? Wouldn't this be a good use of your God-given gifts? If you are the son of God, why not jump from the temple? If you are indeed the son of God, surely no harm will come to you.

When temptation comes to us, does it not often come with the thought we can have it all. We can have whatever we want without having to pay the consequences. We can eat all the desserts we want and still stay thin; we can be constantly on the move and yet be ever more neighborly. We can have an affair and still remain faithful to our spouse. We can stand up for those others deride, refusing to go along with the crowd, and still be popular. We can pray only in times of crises and expect our prayers to be useful and meaningful. With our desire to have it all we often either ignore or refuse to accept any limits. We can eat the apple and jump from the pinnacle and think no harm will befall us.

When temptation comes, it raises the question of our identity. It asks, "Do I see myself in isolation or in relationship. Adam and Eve do not desire relationship with God, but to be like God. When relationship with God is lost sight of, what God wants is no longer important. Jesus, on the other hand, sees beyond his need to eat, his need to connect with God – "Human beings live, not on bread alone, but on every word that proceeds from the mouth of God."

A Seattle newspaper article caught my attention this past week. A woman and her son found a wallet with $2400, credit cards, and a ticket to New Zealand. She and her husband had both lost their jobs and had been living in their car. But unable to keep up the payments, the car had been repossessed and they were currently living in a homeless shelter. Upon finding the wallet, the mother said it seemed like a "God-send", and she was tempted to use the money to purchase two additional tickets for her husband and son, and fly the family to New Zealand. But after wrestling with the temptation to take the money and run, she instead took it to a nearby police station, asking them to return it to its rightful owner. She saw the needs of her family, not in isolation, but in relationship to the needs of the person who had lost the wallet. Her sense of self was not seen in isolation, but in relationship – relationship, not only to her own family's need, but to a stranger's need as well.

This same question of identity faces us when it comes to paying new taxes and passing the upcoming school bond. No one wants new taxes and we would just as soon not be burdened with another school bond, and if we live in isolation, we probably don't need them. But if we are a part of society, then we look not just at our own needs, but at those of society as a whole and the future generations who will follow us.

Temptation also raises the question of identity by asking, "In whom or what do I trust?" When faced with the question of whether to eat the apple, Adam lets Eve make the decision for him, and Eve, in turn, lets the snake tell her what to do. Harvey Cox, who teaches ethics at Harvard and has written about this Adam and Eve story in a recent book, claims that letting the snake tell us what to do is an abdication of our responsibility. By letting others tell us what to do, we put our trust in someone else to make our decisions for us. As our life becomes more complex, there is a temptation for us to abdicate our responsibility to the so called "experts" and let them tell us what to do. But just because technology makes something possible, it doesn't mean it should be done. We can split the atom, but will this knowledge be used to serve the needs of humanity or will it become a weapon of mass destruction.

Sometimes when confronting a problem we are tempted to say, "God will take care of it," but to trust God does not mean we give up our responsibility. Jesus knows that if he jumps from the pinnacle God will not abandon him; but he also knows God will not prevent him from suffering the consequences of his decision. God will never abandon us, but neither will God protect us from our own folly.

There's a story that Martin Luther one time decided not to prepare for a sermon, believing that God would provide inspiration for him to preach when the time came. Afterward, when his wife asked how it went, Martin replied that the Holy Spirit said, "Martin, you're lazy." Our trust in God is not meant to be a blind faith, nor is it meant to relieve us of our own responsibility.

A third way temptation raises the question of our identity is by asking, "Whose interests will I serve?" Adam and Eve find that their interest in increasing their knowledge is in conflict with God's desire that they not eat the apple. And with them, we may well ask, "Is not their desire for knowledge legitimate?" What right, after all, does God have to thwart such a noble desire? And when Jesus is tempted to turn stones into bread, should not his power for good be given its fullest expression? Are not the needs of the hungry worth serving?

Of course, the desire for knowledge is legitimate and the needs of the hungry are worth serving, but both situations need to be seen in a wider context. Does our desire for knowledge go beyond the bounds of what is necessary? Is it excessive? Is it not rather expecting we can serve the interests of God and do whatever we like? Is it not expecting the impossible – like expecting compact cars which are spacious, and luxurious cars which are economical, or expecting everybody to feel free to disagree, yet expecting no one to rock the boat? How can we both revere God and at the same time be God?

Jesus overcomes his temptation to turn stones into bread by serving a stronger passion – his desire to serve God. When temptation comes, we often face not just a choice between "right" and "wrong", but between the "good" and the "better". Feeding the hungry and desiring more knowledge are not bad things in themselves, but they need to be viewed in the context of whose interests are being served. Turning stones into bread to feed the hungry serves a good end, but it does so by turning Jesus into a magician. Jesus may create a following in this way, but it will be based more on himself as a miracle worker than as a faithful servant of God. The focus will be more on himself than on God; more on miracle than faith. Serving our own interests does not always serve the higher interests to which God may call us.

There is an African folktale about a man who asks the most beautiful woman he has ever seen to marry him. She agrees on one condition, telling him, "I have a finely woven basket. Promise not to open it until I give you my permission. If you open it too soon, harm will befall us." He promises, and she marries him.

She places the basket by the door of the house. She is a good wife. She cooks his meals, cleans the house, and even tends his cattle. But as time passes, the man grows curious and wonders, "What does she keep in the basket?" One day he thinks, "What harm will it be if I look? After all, isn't she my wife and isn't it then my basket too?" So the next day when she is out tending the cattle, he opens the basket.

The man begins to laugh, for he sees nothing in her basket. Carefully, he closes it, putting the lid back on just as he has found it. Just then his wife returns home. "What did you do today?" she asks. Laughing, the man answers, "I looked into your basket."

"What did you see?" she asks sadly.

"I saw nothing. It was empty," he says, laughing.

The woman picks up the basket and puts it on her knees. "You saw nothing. But the basket was full. I keep all the beautiful things of the sky in the basket for you and me to share. If you had waited, I would have taught you to see." And with that, she leaves him.

As Adam and Eve are overcome with curiosity and eat of the fruit of the tree of knowledge, so too is this man who opens the basket. On the surface, both instances seem innocent enough, and surely no harm is intended. But in each case, by ignoring what they have been told, they lose out on the joy and delight they might have known.

For each one of us God has a basket of things he wants us to see. Whether we see more than an empty basket depends upon what we do when temptation comes. Will we see only what is in our self interest, or will we see what comes when we take into account our relationship with others and the God who loves us? Will we let someone else tell us what to do, or will we refuse to put God to the test? Like the Jesus we seek to follow, may we choose, not just the good, but the better – that kingdom whose power and glory are forever.

"Coping With Life's Challenges"

"It is by lives that beat in concordance with God that the world will be redeemed" Heschel

The challenges we face in life can come from a variety of sources – both external and internal. The former are things that happen outside our control such as a diagnosis of cancer or some other life-threatening illness, the loss of our home or job, or the defective birth or pre-mature death of a family member. Internal challenges have more to do with how we respond to things like change, conflict, failure, and stress.

It is these later four that will be the focus of this section. Each one of these is a challenge we all face at sometime. Living in a highly competitive, global society we increasingly experience a clash of cultures and values where **conflict** and **failure** seem almost inevitable, and even if we respond in a positive manner, **stress** will be present. Underneath and interwoven in all our living is **change** - the one constant in all our lives.

One of the keys to dealing with failure is to see it in a positive light. Rather than letting it drag us down, it is important to see how failure can become an opportunity for growth. Thomas Edison and Aleksandr Sohzhenitsyn both offer words of wisdom - both in learning what doesn't work and in discovering what matters most in dealing with failure. Looking at how Jesus deals with failure is instructive as well. When we deal with failure in a positive manner it can be seen as a hidden treasure, helping us grow in our humanity while becoming more receptive to the presence of God in our life.

Change is sometimes welcome, but usually it is when we are the one making the change. Most often, however, the struggle to accept change is difficult, especially where it pushes us into unfamiliar territory. Henri Nouwen suggests the most effective way to deal with change is to make the life of the spirit our highest priority. In order to do this, we must first change both the way we listen and the way we see. This entails hearing and seeing everything that happens, not as just one more isolated event, but as one of the rich variety of ways in which God's presence is known.

Our society tends to see conflict as a sign of failure and something to be avoided if at all possible. But in the long run, pretending conflict doesn't exist and withdrawing is not helpful. Resolving conflict in constructive ways begins when we take it seriously and seek to have a positive attitude toward those with whom we disagree. Keeping the level of conflict "issue" specific is important for when the conflict becomes personal, people feel judged and become defensive. In the end, how a conflict is resolved is more important than either winning or losing.

Life will never be without stress. As with failure, not all stress is bad; it can serve a useful purpose. Too much stress can overwhelm us, but without any tension our lives may become pretty dull. The key is finding our proper stress level. Jesus' words in the Sermon on the Mount tell us to "consider the lilies of the field and the birds of the air – they neither sow, nor harvest, nor store in barns, yet God clothes and feeds them". But is it possible for us to put aside our worries and really put our trust in providence? And if it is, how and where do we start?

"When We Fail"

There's an old proverb that says, "Failure, more than anything else in life, determines one's character." What this means, of course, is that failure provides the stage, but what truly determines character is our response. Failures, in and of themselves, are neutral; they may be either stumbling blocks or stepping stones, depending upon how we use them.

A poem that my sixth grade teacher, Mr. Henry, had the class memorize makes it clear who plays the key role when it comes to failure:

You've all that the greatest of men have had;
Two ears, two eyes, two hands to use, if you would be wise.
To each is given when life begins,
A bag of tools, a set of rules.
And each must make, 'er life has flown
A stumbling block or a stepping stone.

This morning's Old Testament story of Cain and Abel contains an important warning. If we don't master our failures, they will master us. When Cain's offering is not accepted, but his brother's is, he feels hurt and angry. Though understandable, his hurt feelings, in and of themselves, are not what kills his brother. It is what he does with them that murders his brother. As Yahweh points out, "Sin is crouching at the door, but you can still master it." Failure is not a sin, but it can, and in Cain's case does, lead to sin.

How can we master failure? Our gospel lesson in Mark suggests two things that may be helpful. First, when our ultimate dream is dashed, let us deal with the task at hand. Jesus' big dream is that his disciples might carry on his ministry, becoming channels of God's love and using their talents to bring peace and healing. This dream, at least in the case of the boy with epilepsy, is obviously dashed, as Jesus learns from the father whose son is afflicted with the illness. Instead of healing his son's epilepsy, the boy's father tells Jesus the disciples have failed to help him.

Obviously disappointed and upset, Jesus shows his exasperation when he asks his disciples, "How much longer must I put up with you? But rather than let his disappointment rule the day, he directs his attention to the boy whom the disciples have failed to help, and rebuking the power that controls the boy's seizures, cures him of his epilepsy. When Jesus fails in his ultimate concern to make men of God out of his disciples, he turns his attention to what he can control, the problem at hand.

Where Jesus directs his anger provides a second thing to remember when dealing with failure. While on the surface it appears Jesus' anger at the disciples is directed at their failure to cure the boy's epilepsy, his deeper concern is not with this outward failure, but rather an inward one – they had lost touch with God. The real failure for the disciples is not that they can't cure the epileptic, but that they failed to pray. No failure can ultimately defeat us so long as we refuse to let it separate us from God.

There are many places in life where we may experience failure. It can occur in an academic pursuit when we fail to pass a required course; it can happen at a job interview when we're not called back; it may be the result of a new recipe that doesn't work out, it may take place on the job when we're passed over for a promotion or let go when the company reorganizes; it may come in a marriage that ends in divorce; or we may experience failure as parents when we ignore or fail to take seriously a child's plea for help. But no matter where or how we may fail, our most important response is to maintain our inner spirit so we hold on to hope.

Maintaining our inner spirit in the midst of failure is seldom easy, but it helps when we see failure, not merely in a negative light, but as something positive. Alexsander Sohzhenitsyn, in his book, The First Circle, writes, "Failures must be seen as hidden treasure for in failure we discover what really matters. What matters is not success or failure but growth, the growth of the human being; not what we are by reason of external achievement, but who we are becoming in terms of the humanity growing within us." The idea that our failures contain hidden treasure can open our eyes to see there is indeed something more valuable than mere success or failure, and that is our growth as human beings. And this kind of growth, which is not limited to our successes, may actually be more forthcoming and more pronounced during times of failure.

Recognizing who we are becoming in our humanity may be aided by recognizing God in our difficulties. Being open to God's presence and realizing that God does not stop loving us when we fail, reminds us we are never alone in dealing with our difficulties and we have resources to call upon that only need to be invited. Paul suggests that the defeated still have everything if they remember they still have God. When he writes in second Corinthians, "We are afflicted in every way, but not crushed; perplexed, but not driven to despair; struck down, but not destroyed," he makes clear what a famous sportswriter, Grantland Rice, once said in much simpler terms, "To be knocked down is no big deal, but to lie there, that's a disgrace." Getting knocked down is a part of entering the ring of life; getting back up is a part of something much bigger – the kind of man or woman we are becoming. For whoever looks to God for direction, faith is always more important than either failure or success.

When Jesus hangs on the cross, his life is a failure to many. In the eyes of those who have hoped he would overthrow their enemies and bring a new kingdom, his refusal to take up a sword is judged to be a failure. In the eyes of his disciples, his life is over and can hardly be deemed a success. But looking at Jesus' life from the standpoint of those who have been led by his spirit over the centuries since, it is hard to call his life a failure. For the millions of persons who have heard his words from the cross, "Father, forgive them for they know not what they do," the cross is not a sign of his defeat, but a source of new life. And for the millions who have heard his call, "Pick up your bed and walk," and found it both healing and empowering, the cross is not a defeat, but simply a step along the way to a new and resurrected life.

As these disparate views illustrate, sometimes what seems to be a failure may merely need time to be termed a success. It was Thomas Edison who said about his many defeats along the way to inventing the light bulb, "I've not failed, I've just found 10,000 ways that won't work." Every detection of what is false may direct us to what is true.

So in summary, let us remember that while failure is a fact of life that can either result in despair or new determination, deepen our resolve or destroy our incentive, it is always an opportunity for growth. And when we maintain our inner spirit, recognizing God in our difficulties, and building upon what we have learned, failure can be like a hidden treasure, opening us up to discover our deepest humanity.

"Coping With Change"

Of all life's challenges, perhaps none is as constant, or everywhere and always present, as change. Wherever we focus, we see change - it is present in both our natural and social environment, and it is a part of our work, family, and church.

As volcanoes erupt, tsunamis and tornadoes sweep across the land, and floods change the course of rivers, the earth's topography is constantly changing. But nature is not the only change agent. Removing rain forests, building dams and flood control projects, we humans are agents of change as well. And with our carbon emissions blackening the air and depleting the ozone layer, we also contribute to global warming, thereby changing our climate, and causing certain species to become extinct and new ones to be born.

New technology continually changes the way we get around and the relationships we have. From horse and buggy to car to plane and space ship, we shorten distance and expand our reach, continually increasing and changing our interactions. From radio to television, from regular mail to e-mail, and from the encyclopedia to Google, we increase the speed of our communication and access to information. And with Face Book and My Space, we widen our contacts, creating relationships with strangers, work for detectives and security specialists, and headaches and worries for parents.

Changes in the work world are no less pronounced. With the increased use of technology and jobs moving from the industrial to the service sector, with outsourcing of work abroad to take advantage of cheap labor, and with the decline of unions, it is no surprise that there is less company loyalty and fewer people spending their working lives with one company. Job dislocation and greedy CEO's wrecking their worker's pensions have greatly increased job change and fostered multi-careers.

And when we retreat to the womb of the family for stability and comfort, little may be found. With one in five families moving every year, one in two marriages ending in divorce, a dramatic increase in the number of single parents, more couples living together outside of marriage, and the increased need for two incomes, the idea of family is undergoing significant change as well. Given these changes, it is easy to identify with the fellow who, when asked by his best man a year after his wedding, "Has your wife changed much? answered, "Yes, she's changed my friends , my habits, and my hours."

In the midst of all these changes, Henri Nouwen may offer the best insight when he says, "The most important change in anyone's life is the change of heart." When Nouwen says the change that matters most is not leaving school, getting married, having children, changing jobs, moving to a new location, being divorced or losing a spouse, it is having a change of heart - what is he getting at?

The Biblical text on which Nouwen stakes his claim is Jesus' statement in the sixth chapter of Matthew where he asks us to move our hearts to the center – what he calls the kingdom of God. When we worry about change, whether it's what we wear or what we should eat, we have our hearts in the wrong place. When, on the other hand, we make the life of the spirit our highest priority – the center of all we think, say, and do – we make the one change that relieves the pressure on all of life's changes.

If this is so, then how do we make this change? How do we make life in the Spirit our highest priority? In simplest terms, this change requires a change in the way we listen and the way we see. For it is here, in our listening and seeing, that we can change from a less self-centered to a more God-centered life.

The importance of changing the way we listen is what Richard Bolles has in mind in his book, The Three Boxes of Life: And How We Get Out of Them. Here he tells the story of two men walking along a crowded, city sidewalk. Suddenly one exclaims, "Listen to the lovely sound of the cricket." Amazed and puzzled, his companion asks, "How can you hear a cricket in the midst of all these people talking and cars whizzing by?" The first man, who is a trained zoologist, had trained himself to listen to the voices of nature. But he didn't explain. He simply took a coin out of his pocket and dropped it to the sidewalk, whereupon twelve people began to look for it. "We hear," he said, "what we listen for."

As Nouwen points out, the center of life for Jesus is his total, uninterrupted listening to God. According to Nouwen, we will never understand the full meaning of Jesus' varied ministry unless we see how the many things he does - healing, teaching, and praying - are all rooted in one thing - listening in love to the One he calls "Father". From his first words to his worried parents when they find him after three days of searching, "Did you not know I must be about my Father's business," to his last words from the cross, "Father, into your hands I commit my spirit," Jesus' primary concern is to do the will of God.

This kind of listening requires a discipline of solitude. Elijah did not encounter God in the earthquake, wind, or fire, but in the still, small voice within. The one journey that ultimately matters is the journey into the place of stillness deep within one's self. If we fail to take time to carve out space for ourselves, we will soon discover that without this discipline, a spiritual life is impossible. Solitude begins with a time and place for God. It means, in Nouwen's words, "being all "ear" for God, listening obediently in God's presence."

The second change necessary for making life in the spirit our highest priority is to change the way we see. This means seeing everything we experience, things, people, events, not as endless cause for worry, but as the rich variety of ways in which God makes his presence known. In this way, everything that happens is not just one more isolated event, but a part of our way to God.

Reading the parables of Jesus, it is easy to see this is the way he looked at life. In the parable of the shepherd looking for the one lost sheep, Jesus sees God's love for the forsaken; in the story of the mustard seed, he sees God's encouragement to those who are discouraged; in the parable of the widow knocking on the judge's door at midnight, he sees God's response to those who persevere; and in the parable of the prodigal son's return, he sees God's patient love, waiting for our return regardless of where we've been.

No where in life is the way we see more important than in the way we see each other. To create space for God requires the constant recognition of the spirit of God in each person we see. Each one of us is like a window, constantly offering each other new views of the mystery of God's presence in our lives. To move from seeing how everything affects <u>me</u> to seeing how it affects <u>us</u> can give a sense of our oneness with all.

Whatever changes surround us in our world today, the most important change in our life is that inner change that we make in our heart – the change in the way we listen and see, so we move from an anxious, self-centered life to a peaceful, trusting, God-centered life and make God's spirit the center of all we think, and do, and say.

"Coping With Conflict"

In our society there seem to be two predominant attitudes toward conflict. On the one hand, it is seen as a sign of failure - something to be feared and avoided at all costs. On the other hand, conflict is seen as inevitable – something that occurs naturally, and when people treat each other with respect, can lead to personal growth.

This morning let us take the later approach, and see conflict as one of the givens of life – the inevitable result of the freedom God gives us. Conflict may be experienced in many of life's arenas. We may find it in the public arena where we debate a school bond issue, or it can occur in the family when parents set bed times for young children and curfews for dating teens. It can also arise in personal decisions in a marriage or relations with fellow workers or the boss. And as we all know, the church can also experience conflict as it deals with certain social issues such as housing the homeless or its stance toward the gay and lesbian communities.

The Bible itself is filled with stories of conflict - Cain and his brother Abel, Jacob and his twin, Esau, David and Saul in the Old Testament, and keeping or abolishing certain Jewish laws in the New Testament. Paul argues in favor of including the circumcised in the faith community, Peter and John are ordered to desist from teaching about Jesus by the Sanhedrin, and Jesus himself engages in numerous disputes with the Pharisees and is often at odds with his own disciples, including Judas, who betrays him.

Wherever conflict may arise, the key is not pretending it doesn't exist and trying to avoid dealing with it, but rather figuring out how it can best be managed so the results are constructive, not destructive. Conflict itself is not something to fear or avoid; it is neither sinful nor unchristian, though how we resolve it may be. With this in mind, let us look at how we may resolve our conflicts so they are constructive and positive, enabling us to grow both personally and as a Christian community.

Perhaps, the first step in dealing with conflict positively is to simply take it seriously. To ignore it exists, to pretend to accommodate someone, to withdraw, or to discount the issue as unimportant are all ways of dealing with conflict that can be destructive. To withdraw or pretend to go along for the sake of keeping the peace may result in hoarding secret hurts and resentments that will very likely erupt at a later date.

When Peter and Barnabas have a disagreement with the church about how converts to the faith are to be circumcised, they go to Jerusalem and discuss the matter with the apostles and elders. Rather than leave the matter unresolved, it is seen as a serious issue that needs to involve a third party. In this cooler climate, it is decided circumcision should not stand in the way of Gentiles who turn to God.

A second step in dealing with conflict is to have a positive attitude toward the person or persons with whom we disagree. Here, it is helpful if we remember that the other person is more important than the issue. Both the circumcised and the uncircumcised are created and redeemed by the grace of God. In God's eyes, all people are worthy of respect and are not to be put down or denigrated when their views differ from our own. Only when people are taken seriously and respected will they feel safe to express their feelings. Unless people are listened to without judgment, there is little chance for a significant change in the relationship and resolution of the conflict.

One way to insure we listen to the other person without judgment is to make sure we keep the level of conflict "issue" specific. Doing so involves an awareness of the three levels of conflict. The first level is the issue itself. In this morning's New Testament story the issue is identified as circumcision, "Should circumcision be required for the Christian?" The second level of conflict is the personal, and it is here that we can easily slide into judging the other person. Staying with circumcision as the issue, it moves to a personal level when one side remarks, "If you think it should be required, you are too inflexible and rigid" and the other side retorts, "If you think it should not be required, you are too wishy-washy and afraid to take a stand." The third level of conflict occurs when the relationship itself is called into question, "If I don't have my way, I'm leaving the church."

Keeping the level of conflict "issue" specific requires us to separate people from issues, while remembering people are always more important than issues. The focus is on the issue, but finding a solution to the conflict never abandons one's concern for how it will affect the other person. Abraham lets Lot settle on the land of his choice because he recognizes that his relationship with Lot is more important than who gets a particular piece of land. If deciding whether circumcision should be a membership requirement for Gentiles entering the Christian community is not to become divisive, it is essential to remember that both the circumcised and the uncircumcised are created and redeemed by God's grace. The "issue" is an important focus, but treating the other person with respect is even more important and can never be abandoned.

Ultimately, the way a conflict is resolved is more important than the outcome. But how can this happen? One helpful way is to put our self in the other person's shoes and not blame them for our problem. What I prefer needs to be expressed, but not idolized; it needs to be seen in the context of the greater good. Just as the batter in baseball who sacrifices the runner on base into scoring position is more concerned about his team's winning than personal glory, so too is the person who sees the one with whom he or she differs, not as the enemy, but as one who offers a point of view that may be a necessary corrective to my own. In this way, a solution that serves not only my interest, but the interest of the greater good, can be found.

While we compete to win in society, in the church we compete to serve, and we serve best when we see the big picture. When taking the lid off a fruit jar one hand turns one way, while the other hand turns the opposite; the objective is not to see which hand wins, but to remove the lid so both hands can enjoy the fruit inside. Too often the question, "Who is winning?" is the focal point of conflict management. If we ask that question, we may win the argument, but lose the personal relationship we value.

Conflict is not bad in and of itself; the key is how we resolve it. If we take it seriously, have a positive attitude about what is possible, keep the level of conflict "issue" specific, and remember that the way it is resolved is more important than winning, then we may experience change not only in how we deal with the issue, but more importantly, with each other.

Jesus resolved the conflict of his life at Gethsemane by yielding his will to God. Is there a better example to follow for we who call ourselves Christian? May the final triumph in the conflicts of life for each of us be found in yielding our will to the One who gives us life and redeems our shortcomings amidst all its challenges.

"Handling Stress: The Challenge of Modern Life"

A recent Harris poll indicates that eighty-nine per cent of all adult Americans report experiencing high stress. Sixty per cent say they feel great stress at least once or twice a week, while thirty per cent report living with high stress nearly every day.

Why are people so tense today? We have a higher standard of living, more leisure time, and a longer life expectancy than any previous generation in America, yet we are in the midst of an epidemic of hypertension. While the possible causes are complex, our pace of life is a major factor. We are a nation on the "go" - one in five families move every year; people have not one, but two or three careers; and one in every two marriages ends in divorce, which creates not one family, but two or three. Any change can create stress, but changing homes, schools, neighborhoods, careers, and families are sometimes almost more than we can handle.

Even though stress may be unavoidable, it is not all bad; it can serve a useful function. A certain amount of stress is essential, not only to avoid boredom, but to bring forth our best efforts. In handling stress, the key is not trying to eliminate it entirely, but to find our optimal stress level – something that varies for each individual. The right amount of stress for one person may be too much for another. The proper level of stress stimulates normal functioning without impairing it - too much stimulation and one withdraws; too little and one is bored. Stress in human life is much like tension on a violin string. If the string has no tension and is slack, no music is heard. If the string is stretched too tightly and it snaps, there is no music. But when the string is under proper tension, beautiful tones result.

How, then, can we find our proper stress level? In that portion of the "Sermon on the Mount" which we heard this morning, we are told to put things in perspective by making sure we put first things first. When Jesus says life is more important than food and the body is more important than clothing he is simply asking us to give thanks for the gift of life and quit worrying about the packaging in which we wrap it - something that came home to me on a recent visit with Oaks Taylor. I asked him how he liked the Insure, which is now his everyday source of nutrition. His answer, "It's not all that tasty, but it keeps me alive," was a good reminder about what things really matter. Oaks knows he's limited in what he can do and eat, but he's still glad to be alive.

When it comes to putting first things first, the story in Luke's gospel about Mary and Martha always rings a bell. When Jesus comes to visit the sisters, Martha busies herself in the kitchen preparing something for him to eat, while Mary sits down and listens to Jesus talk about his day. Upset that her sister is not helping her, Martha complains to Jesus and asks his sympathy for having to do the work by herself. Imagine how shocked she must have been when Jesus tells her she worries about too many things, and what Mary has chosen is best. Providing something for our guests to eat is a gracious thing to do, but sometimes simply being personally present is more important, and a whole lot less stressful.

None of us like to play Martha's part in the world - at least not where it involves the whiney, complainer. But I must confess that's exactly where I found myself during our last move. We had just made our last trip, carrying boxes of our belongings to our house and I was anxious to get them unpacked and put away. Carrying boxes upstairs to our bedroom, I noticed Pat and our daughter, Jennifer, sitting on the floor engaged in lively conversation. Each time I carried a box upstairs and saw them still taking a break, I became more and more annoyed; the Martha in me growing more frustrated with each box. Tired and angry, I could have used a break myself, but instead of sitting down with them, I silently seethed at the injustice – while I did the work, they sat on their fannies and talked. Of course, at the time I didn't see the Martha in myself. Only much later, after I spewed some things that would have been better left unsaid, did I recognize who was really putting first things first.

Trusting providence to provide what we need goes against the grain of the American work ethic. We relate more easily to "God helps those who help themselves" than we do to, "Consider the birds of the air…they neither sow nor harvest nor store in barns, yet God feeds them." But the point Jesus is making is not that the birds do not work, but that they do not worry. If God feeds them, how much more will he care for us? Ultimately, neither work nor worry can provide our bread, but only the goodness of God. As Martin Luther noted in his commentary on this text, "Birds may fly and hop all over the world, but where God has not put, none will feed." Trusting God will provide does not mean doing nothing, but it does mean we don't get stressed worrying about the outcome.

It has been said that perception is in the middle between external conditions that worry us and our internal attitude. Life, in this situation, is a process of choosing sides – will we concentrate more on what lies beyond us or will our focus be on what lies within us. The former is something we have little influence over; the latter is always in our hands and has the capacity to either heighten or diminish the power of that which lies beyond. We can get so stressed about a coming exam or a house mortgage or a son or daughter's marriage that we lose sleep or we can prepare for the exam, pay what we can, hold our child's marriage in prayer, and trust that whatever happens, it will still be in God's loving hands.

When Jesus says, "Seek first the kingdom of God and his righteousness, and all these things shall be yours as well," he is telling us something we already know – our anxiety level is reduced when we get our values and commitments straight. As our teenagers sometimes show us, and when we remember our own love stories, a great love can drive out every other concern. Sometimes when our finance committee sets the annual budget, it is determined almost entirely by what is pledged. While this may be sound financially, I wonder what might happen were we to see the budget more in terms of what God calls us to do. If our highest commitment is to do God's bidding, might not our finance drive tell us a different, and less stressful story?

In the end, Jesus reminds us we are not to worry about tomorrow for tomorrow will take care of itself. "Each day," he wisely acknowledges, "has enough troubles of its own." Following in this vein, someone has observed, "There are two days in every week about which we should not worry; one is yesterday, and the other is tomorrow." If we are to find our optimal level of stress, we might well begin by limiting our worries to the day we are living.

Life will never be without stress. The question will always be, not is it present, but how are we handling it. Jesus tells us things will always go better if we put first things first, trust God, seek his kingdom above all else, and live one day at a time. It is, I believe, the way not only to peace, but to a more healthy and productive life.

"Coping With Our Emotions"

Emotion is the bud, not the flower, and is of no value unless it expands into the flower. Murray

Our emotions are an important part of who we are. Without emotion, life loses excitement and passion, our tears dry up, and our laughter vanishes; the inflection in our voice goes flat, our eyes grow dull, and our actions become more like robots, rigid and mechanical. With emotion, we can sing and dance and joyfully celebrate friendship and family and the successes and triumphs we attain.

But while our deepest feelings can move us to compassion that results in acts of justice and mercy, strong feelings, when unchecked, can also blind us to reality and lead to acts of violence and destruction. How can we tap into our emotions so they serve our best interests? How can we use the energy our emotions generate in positive ways?

The four sermons in this chapter deal with four of our most basic emotions – fear, anger, envy, and self-pity. While on the surface none of these are commonly seen as positive emotions, fear and anger can both be used in positive ways. Envy and self-pity are important emotions to identify since they can be quite destructive if not reigned in.

Of all human emotions, perhaps none is more difficult to admit than envy. As a result, it wears many disguises. At its heart, envy arises from comparing ourselves to someone else. When our focus is on another person, our energy is not available for our own development. How can we overcome this diverted attention, and learn to stay at home with ourselves? How we can offer our own gifts without looking at another's?

Fear is an elemental, God-given emotion that surrounds much of our lives. It serves a positive purpose in alerting us to potential dangers, but not all fear is positive. Whenever we exaggerate the danger, fear is not healthy. Separating normal fear from exaggerated fear is a first step in coping with fear; later, however, our faith becomes the critical factor. Learning to walk in faith has a lot to do with whether we view God as a Judge and Law-Giver or as a Loving Parent – the first fosters fear; the latter breeds confidence and trust.

Anger is a very normal and necessary part of every person's life. It can be either a constructive or destructive force depending upon whether it is accepted and owned, and how it is used. Anger denied usually erupts in destructive ways; when it is ventilated it has a chance to move toward something more positive. Distinguishing between feelings and facts can play a positive role in accepting the presence of anger. Anger directed toward injustice is never misplaced, but we need to be sure the injustice is real .and not just an excuse for being self-indulgent.

Self-pity results when we refuse to say "yes" to life when it hasn't turned out as we thought it should. Getting beyond self-pity has a lot to do with how we see ourselves, how we view the past, and the way we look at suffering. Feeling sorry for ourselves most often happens when we see ourselves as victims of some misfortune and feel we are locked into the past and suffering unjustly. Whether we continue to suffer depends upon our willingness to transcend this self-image and create a different picture of our past and learn from our suffering.

"The Envious Heart"

A couple of weeks ago at a recognition dinner for one of our community leaders, I overheard one of his business rivals who was seated across the table from me, say in an overly-loud voice, "If it hadn't been for his father giving him the business, he never would have made it." This not-so-subtle criticism is but one of the many faces of envy.

The faces of envy are many and easy to recognize when the speaker is discounting someone else's accomplishments or questioning their recognition. If you've ever heard any of the following comments, you have been given a picture of some of envy's other faces: "She wouldn't have so many friends if it weren't for her money." "It helps to *m*arry the boss's daughter." "She wouldn't have even been hired if she wasn't so good looking." Or, "Now we know who the boss is sleeping with."

Of all human emotions, perhaps none is more difficult to admit. Envy is not something we like to confess; hence, it wears many disguises. Recognizing one of these disguises, the political philosopher, Thomas Hobbes, once observed, "The praise of ancient authors proceeds not from reverence of the dead, but from envy of the living." In praising the dead one can shine the light on those who are less threatening and keep the living in the shadows.

At the heart of envy is comparison. The focus of the envious heart is always on the other person so that his or her achievements become all important. When the women celebrated David's victory over Goliath singing, "Saul has killed his thousands, and David his tens of thousands," Saul was displeased that David had been given more credit and his jealously of David blossomed from that day on. When Jesus asks Peter to follow him, Peter looks at John and asks Jesus, "What about him?" For Peter, what John does occupies his attention so much it gets in the way of his commitment to Jesus. His focus is more on John than on the one who has requested his support.

When our focus is on someone else, the energy spent watching or copying them is not available for developing our own unique gifts, and it often leads to self-abandonment. When a young man asked the poet, Rilke, what he must do to become a great writer, Rilke is reported to have said, "Quit trying to copy someone else's style, and simply develop your own."

Every person has his or her own unique role to play in life. As our children's talk made clear, ink pens come in a variety of styles, colors, and sizes, but they each are equally adept at conveying their author's thoughts when given a chance. They need not adopt another's pens looks in order to serve their function. No one's gifts are impaired by the gifts of another.

It is easy to be threatened by another's gifts, especially when they seem so abundant in comparison to our own. But it is only when we learn to stay at home with ourselves and give what **we** have to give without looking over our shoulder that we will not be threatened by what others have to give.

Envy can easily breed a spirit of just demands, and set up a system of bookkeeping – if they got that, then I should get the same. When Joseph's father had a multi-colored tunic made for him to wear, his brothers felt they should get one too. Have you ever seen children at a birthday party argue over who got the biggest piece of cake? Sometimes this system of bookkeeping happens in a marriage when the husband feels he must get a new fishing rod or set of golf clubs because his wife got a new set of clothes, or the wife feels she must buy a new car because the husband got a new boat. When this spirit of just demands is present, it is no surprise to find siblings arguing over the division of an inheritance and professional athletes demanding a new contract when a team mate signs a new deal at a higher figure.

To combat this "keeping-up-with-the-Jones" attitude it is helpful to focus on quality, not equality. The renowned psychologist, Dr. Haim Ginott in his classic book, Between Parent And Child, says, "Children do not yearn for equal shares of love, but rather the uniqueness of their relationship." Children need to be loved uniquely, not uniformly. If we want to avoid creating envy in our children, it is important that we convey the uniqueness of our relationship, not its fairness or sameness. We may love one child for her independent spirit; the other for her sensitivity to others; one child for his athletic prowess, and another for his intellectual curiosity.

In addition to leading to self-abandonment and a spirit of just demands, envy can also make us think in terms of privileges instead of responsibilities. We look at what others have that we don't, and become jealous. We think of the fame and wealth of the famous actor or entertainer, and think how nice it would be to have such a devoted following. But few of us realize how much of their time in public is not their own; they are constantly having to be "on" and everything they do and say is under a microscope. Most famous people complain about how little time they have to simply be themselves, and many ask themselves if their celebrity status is worth it.

When we learn to think in terms of responsibilities and not privileges, then we will think not in terms of what others have that we don't, but what we have that others are without. Had Joseph kept his dreams to himself and looked at them in terms of his responsibilities instead of using them to emphasize his exalted position in the family, his brothers might not have been so inclined to throw him in the well and sell him to the Ishmaelites. A little humility might have made it easier to get along with his brothers and kept him out of slavery.

In a similar vein, the eldest son in the parable of the Prodigal Son might have joined with his father in celebrating his younger brother's return had he remembered the rich companionship and abundant privileges he had enjoyed with his father during his brother's absence. He saw the killing of the fatted calf and party being thrown for his brother as a privilege that should have been his and lost sight of the reward of being his father's constant companion that had accrued to him by simply tending to his responsibilities on the farm.

Let us live out our lives where we find them, tending to the responsibilities that are ours and not comparing what we have to our neighbors. Like Peter and John, we are each given different functions and responsibilities. But these differences do not make us greater or less than another; we who would seek to honor what God has given us are simply called to celebrate and use our unique gifts to the best of our ability. As Jesus said to Peter, "Never mind the task given to someone else. Your job is to follow me." Our glory is never in comparison to someone else; it is in loving and serving God as Christ does without worrying about what advantages or rewards another may receive.

"Coping With Our Fears"

In one form or another, fear dogs all of us. In childhood, it's the fear of going to bed, or as with my granddaughters, fear of the basement; later it may be fear of school or of not making the team; still later, it's fear of not getting into a certain college or fear of flunking out; and once we're out, it's fear of not getting the job or fear of getting laid off and not being able to pay our bills. And on a larger scale, it's fear of a terrorist attack, or a recession, or an environmental catastrophe. As long as we're living, it seems there's always something to fear; fear is omnipresent.

Perhaps, this is why Jesus talked so much about it. It would be hard to find a statement in the New Testament more characteristic of Jesus than the command, "Be not afraid." To the worried multitudes, he says, "Be not anxious." When he enters a house of mourning, his first words are, "Fear not, only believe." To his frightened followers on a storm-tossed vessel come the calming words, "It is I; be not afraid." And at his last meal with the disciples before his crucifixion, John's gospel reports him saying, "Let not your hearts be troubled; neither let them be afraid."

Undoubtedly, Christ directed himself to fear because he saw it surrounded so much of people's lives. The fear of the disciples in the storm-tossed sea was certainly real, but no less real than the fears that plague so many people today. The fear of terrorism, the fear of losing one's home or being incapacitated, the fear of losing a spouse to cancer, and fear of financial reversal are just as real for people living today.

Fear is an elemental, God-given emotion and therefore has a constructive and essential purpose. It is like a warning light that cautions us to be prepared and take appropriate steps to deal with a potential danger. Thus, we have first-alert weather reports, tsunami warnings, building codes designed to withstand high stress, counseling and support groups for cancer survivors and single parents, drugs to combat bi-polar disorders and other illnesses, and insurance and federal relief programs to aid in times of disaster.

But despite these efforts to help us deal with our fears, fear still causes many people to needlessly lose sleep. How can we cope with our fears in a constructive, Christian way? Without pretending to have all the answers, let me suggest some steps that may be helpful.

First, let us sort out normal from exaggerated fear. Normal fear is innate and cautions us to be careful when walking on a high ledge; exaggerated fear makes mountains out of mole hills. Education consists in being afraid at the right time. Charles Spurgeon, an influential 19th century, British preacher and writer, tells the story of a time he gave a sack of groceries and some money for rent to one of his parishioners with instructions to give it to a widower whom he knew needed it. But the widower, hearing the knock on her door and thinking it might be a bill collector, refused to come to the door. Not sure what to do, the man left the money and groceries at the door. The widow who feared the worst, never got the gift - it was taken by someone who felt his need was just as great and wasn't worried about being found out. .

A healthy fear makes us keep our distance from pit bulls and rattlesnakes; a phobia keeps us petrified at the sight of a cocker spaniel and a garter snake. A healthy fear makes us refuse to drive with someone who has been drinking; a phobia keeps us from even taking driving lessons. A healthy fear alerts us to not let children play with matches; a phobia is when we refuse to get a baby sitter for fear something bad might happen.

Our fears always outnumber our real dangers. An Arab folk tale tells about a plague that swept across the country. Sent to assess the situation, the king's messenger returns to report ten thousand deaths. Astonished, the king asks, "You mean the plague took that many lives." "No," his messenger replied, "the plague killed 5,000; fear took the rest."

When the letter of John says, "In love there is no room for fear; perfect love drives out fear," the author alludes to the power of love in combating our fears. One crucial aspect of this is having confidence in God's love. But where can this kind of confidence come from? A look at Jesus' Sermon on the Mount is helpful.

A fundamental basis of Jesus' response to fear is his belief that the world belongs to God, and we are all children of God. In the Sermon on the Mount, Jesus helps us understand what this means when he asks, "Is there anyone among you who would hand his son a stone when he asks for bread?" Jesus makes it clear that if we know how to give our children what is good, how much more will God give good gifts to those who ask him. And, he continues, "If God sees that the birds of the field have sufficient food and the lilies of the field are clothed, will he not much more look after our needs?"

Jesus assures us that what God has given us will continue to come. In the final analysis, neither work nor anxiety can secure our daily bread, for bread is a gift of our Creator. Birds and flowers glorify God, not by their industry and toil, but by their unquestioning acceptance of God's gifts. True, that bird who does not search for food will die of hunger, but the bird finds food not only as a result of searching, but primarily owing to the goodness of God – where God has not put, no one finds, even though the whole world should work itself to death.

Confidence in God's love belongs to those who walk in faith, not fear. It has been said that fear is characteristic of someone who expects to be punished. If so, so long as we regard God as Judge and Law-Giver, good deeds will be seen as our "protection" payment to safeguard us from harm. But when God is seen as love, there is no need for such payments – God's love is freely given, and not based on our good deeds, but on God's compassion alone.

Helmut Thielicke, a German theologian and preacher, tells the story in his book, Christ and the Meaning of Life, about a mother and her four-year old son, riding on a ferry in a stormy night. A passenger seated across the way notices the child seems totally oblivious to the danger and asks the child, "Aren't you afraid when the boat tips like this?" "No," shot back the four-year-old, "My daddy's the captain." For the boy, there was no need to worry since the boat was in his father's hands. Cannot we say the same when it comes to our troubled world and the One whose love oversees it?

When the gospels report that Christ calmed the seas may it not so much refer to Christ actually stopping a storm, but rather that wherever Christ is, the storms of our life are indeed calmed. To journey with Christ is to journey in peace even in a storm. Perhaps, our real tragedy is not that we do not know how to cope with our fears, but that so often we fail to ask God's guidance and trust God's goodness.

"Coping With Our Anger"

Anger is a very normal and necessary part of every person's life. It can also be a very productive force for good. For us to see anger in a positive light may seem contrary to our usual upbringing and Christian teaching, but this morning's New Testament reading should remind us that anger was not foreign to our Lord. It was anger that led Christ to drive the money changers out of the temple.

Anger, like other human emotions, can be constructive, depending upon its use. As the Greek philosopher, Aristotle, told his compatriots in the third century before Christ, "Anybody can become angry – that is easy; but to be angry at the right time, for the right purpose, and in the right way – that is hard." There is a time and a place for everything, including anger. The key is knowing the right time and the right way.

The first step in dealing with anger is to recognize and admit it. When we go storming around the house and our spouse asks, "What's wrong?" "Nothing." is not a very good answer. Anger cannot be destroyed or denied; it will eventually come out and usually not in a good way when it has been denied. Sometimes anger that is denied comes out in over-eating; sometimes in headaches and lack of sleep; and occasionally in strokes and depression. It's no fun being around someone trying to repress their anger, so most people and especially dogs, try and stay out of the way since they never know when they may be the recipient of an angry outburst.

When we use energy to put down anger, we must also expend energy to keep it down. This kind of effort depletes the energy needed to express other feelings. It is no surprise when psychologists tell us it is only when people are allowed to express negative feelings and get them out of their system that positive feelings can take their place. As Paul's letter to the Ephesians says, "Never let the sun set on your anger."

When anger is ventilated it has a chance to move toward something more positive, but when it is concealed, it can harden into revenge. One such instance occurred recently when someone I know was not invited to be in her sister's wedding party. She felt slighted and her anger showed, but rather than admit it, she refused to go to the house-warming for the newlyweds when they returned from their honeymoon. Now an even bigger barrier exists between the sisters, and where before there was only one angry sister, now there are two.

One thing that may help us accept the presence of anger is to distinguish between feelings and acts. Angry feelings need not become hurtful acts. Is not this what the letter to the Ephesians suggests when it says,

"Even if you are angry, do not sin." When a child says, "I hate you," our first response is often to scold the child and have them say they're sorry. But this kind of response may only encourage the child to be dishonest and deny his true feelings. Real acceptance of the child's feelings, on the other hand, may open the door for the child to vent her feelings and help her deal with them more positively. Feelings in themselves are not bad; anger does not kill; people do. We need a world without violence; not a world without anger.

In the movie, Children of a Lesser God, one of the deaf students calls the teacher a "meathead" and is affirmed. While many of us might find the child out of line and call for some kind of reprimand, in the movie the child is affirmed because the teacher recognizes the response is more a reflection of the child's frustration at not being understood than a denigration of the teacher. While failure to understand what is behind someone's anger can and often does exacerbate the problem, seeing what lies behind the anger may lead to a deeper understanding, better communication, and in some cases, even healing.

Understanding what may lie behind someone's anger is not always easy, especially since anger is sometimes confused with another primary feeling. Dr. Thomas Gordon, a clinical psychologist who was instrumental in starting Parent-Effectiveness Training, emphasizes that anger is often a secondary feeling. An angry outburst from a child who unexpectedly comes home to an empty house may be a secondary feeling; the primary feeling may be fear or a sense of abandonment. A parent who gets angry when a child leaves his coat at school may be unaware that at a deeper level she's feeling a sense of failure at not having enough money to buy a replacement. If we can identify the primary feeling that often underlies our anger, we may have a better handle on coming to grips with our anger, and in turn, be able to make a more appropriate response.

Anger, however, should not be glamorized when it is merely self-indulgence. When Christ is criticized for his ministry and called a wine-bibber and a glutton, he remains silent, but when the Pharisees refuse to help someone who is hurt merely because they feel it is the wrong day of the week, he is indignant and his anger flows freely. To express anger because his ministry is misunderstood would have been self indulgent and a waste of energy, but to voice his anger at human indifference to suffering is indeed something to be angry about for it is a reflection of God's anger.

It is important that we distinguish between someone throwing his golf club when he hits a bad shot and someone else being upset over child prostitution. The former is like being upset because your favorite television show is preempted, and while it may be frustrating; it hardly calls for anger; the latter, on the other hand, is an abuse of those who are least able to defend themselves and should never be tolerated.

There are plenty of injustices in this world about which anger is never misplaced. When medical insurance is denied someone because of a so-called pre-condition or hospital care is denied someone because of the color of their skin; when public officials take bribes and police officers and priests abuse their authority; when people go to bed hungry, and governments subsidize landowners for keeping their fields out of production; when women with more experience and qualifications are paid less for doing the same work as men and passed over for a promotion by the same men; and when anyone in authority harasses those whom they supervise, we all have not only a right, but a duty to be angry and work to correct the abuse.

However, in any instance where anger is an appropriate response, it is important that the purpose of our anger be clear. Our anger should not simply be an excuse for us to vent our emotions or castigate and intimidate those whom we don't like. Rather, our anger should please God by serving the bigger purpose of helping to correct an injustice, holding those responsible for the injustice accountable for what they have done and bringing justice, comfort, and healing to the victims.

In conclusion, let us remember that anger is neither to be feared nor abused. It can be a great teacher, informing us what things we care enough about to get upset. When they are petty, we can learn to ask forgiveness; when they are continuous, we can learn patience; and when they are serious we can use our anger to help correct injustice and bring healing to the victims.

"Self-Pity: The Enemy Within"

Have you ever felt sorry for yourself? If you're like most people, the answer is no doubt "*yes*". A recent magazine survey suggests five out of five people have experienced self-pity at sometime in the past year.

While we may not always be in touch with feelings of self-pity, it is relatively easy to identify them if we are simply alert to the words or feeling, "If only..." If only I had gotten that promotion, we would have the money and be out of debt. If only she could understand what it means to me, she would go along with our move and we could buy the house we really want. If only he knew how much I've sacrificed, he wouldn't think like that. If only she had agreed to counseling, we wouldn't be divorced.

In all of these "if only" statements there is a basic feeling we have not been given our due; we are misunderstood and under-appreciated. There is a sense with all these feelings of self-pity that life is unjust, and we are the victims of circumstances beyond our control. Elizabeth O'Connor, in her book, Our Many Selves, says, "Self-pity results when we refuse to say "yes" to life, especially when it hasn't turned out as we thought it would." There are, of course, times when we need to refuse to say "yes" to what is, but the question is, "When, and how do we say it?"

Saying "yes" to disappointment is never a good thing when appropriate feelings, such as grief and sadness, have been repressed. Grief is a normal and necessary part of our being able to move on with our life after someone dies or a dream has been shattered. But while a period of grieving is necessary, to hold on to suffering past its due is to have an idolatry in one's life. Suffering that is not given up narrows and restricts our life.

The Biblical story of Jonah is a case in point. Because he feels the postponement of Nineveh's destruction has betrayed him, he feels sorry for himself and even asks God to take his life. But God refuses, explaining that Jonah's understanding of God is too restricted – he sees only God's judgment, but not God's mercy. Hence, Jonah's faith in God is neither deepened nor enlarged.

It is an important part of life to make plans and have dreams. But when these plans and dreams are not realized, or don't work out according to our expectation, there comes a time when we need to give them up. If we cling too long to the old, continually reviewing in our minds what might have been, we may simply preserve a gnawing sense of emptiness and resentment.

This may have been what happened to Judas. He did not grasp the concept of the Messiah as the suffering servant and, like so many in his day, clung to old political expectations that the Kingdom of God should be ushered in with swords. Disappointed that Jesus would not take up the sword, and continuing to hold to the idea that he should, Judas cannot perceive and enter into the new world that Jesus is bringing about through a more peaceful means.

Getting beyond self-pity is never easy, but there are ways we can deal with such feelings that can make a difference. One thing that comes to mind immediately is how we see ourselves. Overcoming self-pity involves moving from seeing one's self as victim to seeing one's self as creator. When we see ourselves as victim our tendency is to look to someone else for answers. Jonah feels sad because his feelings are tied to Ninevah's fate and the climbing gourd; whatever happens to them determines how he feels. Thus, his life is controlled by external circumstances.

The man lying by the pool in John's gospel, however, comes to see that his life is not in someone else's hands, but his own. He has been ill for thirty-eight years, but when Jesus tells him to pick up his bed and walk, he decides to stop waiting for someone else to carry him to the pool of healing waters, and puts himself into the pool. As long as he sees himself as a victim, he waits for someone else to come to his aid. But when he realizes his life is not dependent upon someone else, he takes charge of things himself and instead of remaining a victim becomes a creator of a new life and is healed.

The way we view the past is another important element in helping us move beyond self-pity. Do we feel locked into our past or can we learn from the past? Jonah can't see God's grace because he's locked into the past, seeing only what could have been. To hang onto what might have been, not only locks us into the past, but robs us of the future so that instead of becoming creators, we become victims.

S.I. Hayakawa, a well-known linguist, tells the story in his book, Symbol, Status and Personality, about a time when he lived near the Indiana Avenue streetcar line in Chicago. The street was often blocked by badly parked cars and huge trailer trucks backing into warehouses and maneuvering in everybody's way. Some streetcar drivers seemed to expect to be able to drive down the street without interruption. Every time they got blocked, they would get steamed up, clang their bells, and lean out their cars to shout obscenities. Other streetcar drivers, however, seemed to expect delays – a realistic expectation, because they usually happened. And they could sit and wait without impatience, cleaning their fingernails, writing their reports, or reading the paper. In other words, confronting the same situation, some of the drivers, locked into their false expectation that their should be no delays, fell into a rage; others, who had learned from the past, simply enjoyed using the delay as a time to relax and fill in their reports.

A third important factor in overcoming self-pity has to do with suffering – whether we fight against it or accept and live through it. Graham Howe, author of The Open Way, says, "Nothing can be done about feelings of self-pity until we have first accepted them." This does not mean we grow indifferent to them, but it does mean we are willing to suffer and learn what they have to teach. When Christ accepts his suffering and lives through it, not refusing and fighting against it, it becomes transmuted. It is absorbed and becomes a part of his journey to God.

Elizabeth O'Connor, who writes about suffering in her book, Our Many Selves, sounds a similar note when she claims, "The most tragic thing that can happen is when someone suffers all their life and never knows a higher level of life for it." As she notes, "Suffering can either bring us closer to God or separate us from God." In either case, every moment of suffering is an opportunity for growth.

The recognition in life that some elements and aspects of the given cannot be changed may lead us toward the view that the given as a whole is unchangeable. But if we are willing to see it, there is almost always an area of freedom available when we refuse to wallow in self-pity. There are ghosts of the past that haunt the crossroads of all our lives, telling us what might have been, holding us to the past, and restricting our future. Whether we shall be crippled by these ghosts or freed from them depends to a great extent upon whether we choose to be their victims or creators; whether we learn from the past and are able to accept our suffering and come to know a higher level of life for it. May we all choose to be, not victims, but creators of new life!

"Social Justice and Global Concerns"

"Justice is the constant desire and effort to give every person his or her due." Justinian

Confronting injustice was central to Jesus ministry and one of the things I've most admired about his life. His compassion for the least, whether feeding the hungry, healing the sick, or reaching out to the outcast is offered without reservation and regardless of the cost or opposition.

As a Christian minister, I felt the church was called to follow Jesus' example, reaching out to those in need in its own community, acting as an advocate for the needy and an agent for social change. Hence, meeting social needs was always a high priority in my ministry. In Monroe, it meant establishing a recycling center, visiting residents and setting up a day care center at the Monroe Reformatory so wives could leave their children while visiting spouses. At Green Lake it involved workshops on retirement and death and dying, and bringing in skilled tradesmen to demonstrate how to do home remodeling projects. In Puyallup, the church helped set up a peace conference, planted potatoes to help feed the hungry, and offered college scholarships. Back in Seattle, the priority was working with the homeless - housing them in the church basement at Woodland Park, and furnishing transitional apartments for them at Sand Point.

Owing to the often controversial nature of social justice issues, one thing I tried to avoid in these sermons was being moralistic, assuming people needed to be educated and telling them what they ought to do. Two things I found helpful were identifying with lay persons in acknowledging my own difficulties dealing with an issue and using dialogue sermons with people directly affected by an issue, bringing in a gay priest, a Muslim, a student protestor, and a homeless person on different occasions. It also helped to combine these sermons with a study group focusing on the issue being addressed.

Though the sermons dealing with social issues cover a wide range of subjects, ranging from Jesus and politics to gun control, peace and prejudice, those included here deal with AIDS, hunger, environmental stewardship, God and the space age, and the interplay of technological innovation and quality of life issues. Wherever possible, these sermons became springboards for greater church involvement. In the case of AIDS, a person with AIDS shared its impact on his life and offered ways people could help make a difference, which led to some church members working directly with the local AIDS alliance group. Responding to the issue of hunger, people worked in food banks, tended our potato patch, and set up breakfasts for the homeless. Environmental issues were addressed with a study group that set up the recycling center in Monroe and an environmental task force at Light of the Hill provided weekly suggestions in the church bulletin, listing ways individuals could be more environmentally responsible. Science and religion issues were dealt with in a series of forums where medical people discussed vitro fertilization and euthanasia, and agricultural agents talked about genetic manipulation of crops. Though there was no structured response to the sermon on technology and quality of life issues, it did lead some people to eliminate tv dinners and cut out fast-food stops, while others said they decided to limit their e-mail responses to once a week and monitor more closely the tv viewing habits and computer use of both their children and themselves.

"Standing Up For the Least"

It is an embarrassing situation, growing more uncomfortable by the minute. It is supposed to be a quiet, dinner party. Simon has invited several of his friends. Jesus, the miracle-worker and healer, is the guest of honor.

A pleasant evening for the occasion, they are just sitting down to enjoy the meal when she appears. It is obvious by her shabby dress that she is not the kind of person who would ever in a million years be invited to such a party. Luke says she has a bad name in town, which probably means she is a prostitute – a woman of the streets. She is certainly not the kind of woman one invites home to meet the family.

To crash the party as she does most likely means one of two things: either she doesn't care what people think or her needs are so great it no longer matters. Whatever the case, she sits down next to Jesus, tears streaming down her face, onto Jesus' feet. Everybody looks without trying to make it obvious.

Now she wipes his feet with her hair – people look the other way. Now she anoints his feet with myrrh, and as if that isn't enough, begins kissing them. No one says anything; not the woman, not Jesus, and not any of the guests. Simon is the host – it's his house; his dinner party. Why doesn't he do something? The silence is becoming unbearable.

But what should <u>he</u> do? It is Jesus' feet that she is touching, yet he doesn't say anything, and he doesn't even seem to mind. Is he naïve or simply too embarrassed and polite to say something. Surely, Simon reasons, if he is a man of God, he knows about her kind. Surely he will say something. And so Simon, not wishing to make a further scene, sits in silent judgment.

Before we delve further into this story, let's shift our focus to a more contemporary setting. It concerns a boy who has been diagnosed with AIDS – for many, the modern equivalent of leprosy. This story has made headlines all across the country. Ryan White, the first known school child to contact AIDS, is returning to school. During the coffee break at work, several parents are discussing his return.

A woman named Ann begins, "Well, I can sympathize with Ryan and his family, but I don't blame other parents for holding out their kids. Who wants to take a chance like that."

Her friend, Mary, looks at it differently, and asks, "What chance? It can only be transmitted by sexual contact, contaminated needles, or contact with infected blood – I don't see how anything like that can happen at school."

Ann, however, stands her ground. "Well, maybe not, but we're not taking any chances. We've already enrolled our Jimmy in St. Andrew's Christian School."

A third mother, Jo, enters the conversation. "I can appreciate what you're doing, but don't you think that's a bit drastic. What happens if someone there has the AIDS virus and no one even knows about it?"

"It seems to me," Mary adds, rejoining the conversation, "Ryan is being punished for something he had no responsibility for, and sending our kids elsewhere is only going to create more hysteria and division in our community."

Remembering Sunday's worship service, Jo reports, "Last Sunday our pastor read a letter from the Bishops, saying we are supposed to be Christ's healing presence in the AIDS crisis. But my husband and I aren't sure what that means."

Mary considers the question and adds her own, "I'm not sure either. What do you think someone like Christ would do?"

Mary's question is one we might all be asking. Like the woman who is anointing Jesus' feet with her tears, Ryan White is for many people today, not only someone creating an embarrassing situation, but someone to avoid. He doesn't have leprosy, but to many he is considered an outcast and someone to stay away from.

Now let's get back to Simon's dinner party, which we left a few minutes ago. It just may offer us an idea how Jesus would respond to Ryan's situation today. Let's re-visit the story and see where it goes.

All eyes turn to Jesus. The woman has not gone away. She continues to rub the myrrh on his feet. As last, Jesus speaks. But it's not to the woman, but to Simon on her behalf. He tells a story about two debtors – one who owes five hundred pieces of silver and one who owes fifty, and asks Simon, "Which one would be most grateful if their debts were forgiven?"

The answer seems obvious, and Simon replies, "The one who is let off more." Jesus says, "You are right" and then, turning to the woman, adds, "You see this woman, Simon? I came into your house, and you poured no water over my feet, but she has poured out her tears over my feet and wiped them away with her hair. You gave me no kiss, but she has been covering my feet with kisses ever since I came in. You did not anoint my head with oil, but she has anointed my feet with ointment. For this reason I tell you that her sins, many as they are, have been forgiven her, because she has shown such great love." Then he said to the woman, "Your sins are forgiven."

Jesus not only comes to the defense of the woman, he becomes her advocate. Why? Does he simply have a bias toward the under-dog and the outcast? There is ample evidence that he does, but I think it has more to do with the way he sees people; Jesus sees with the eyes of grace, not judgment.

Where Simon looks at the woman's past, and dismisses her as a sinner; Jesus looks at her past, and sees her pain and need for understanding and acceptance. Where Simon looks at her behavior and sees an intrusion and an embarrassment; Jesus sees what she does as an act of kindness and love.

A news reporter recently interviewed a member of our community who was living with AIDS. When asked, what he found to be the most difficult thing about living with AIDS, the man replied, "The loneliness – my wife, my kids, my parents, and my fellow workers have all abandoned me."

Jesus stands up for the least, not just because the sick need a doctor, but because he sees their pain and knows it is more important to respond to their pain than remain aloof, safe in the knowledge of his own good health. Jesus stands up for the least because responding to human need for healing is more important than observing social graces.

Simon assumed he knew the woman better than Jesus; but he only saw her as a sinner, not as one whom God loves. He has forgotten that no one is righteous in God's sight. Standing up for the least begins with remembering we all stand equally in need of God's grace. Yet, there is not one of us whom God is not ready to forgive.

Where does this freedom to see like Jesus come from? Perhaps, from remembering: (1) every person is a creature of God and an object of God's love, (2) even the most shameless sinner can be forgiven, and (3) no one is righteous in God's sight; all of us stand equally in need of God's grace and forgiveness.

“The Christian and Hunger”

What is hunger? To most Americans it is a mild discomfort, quickly alleviated, but to forty per cent of the world it is a gnawing feeling in the stomach that turns into what Mahatma Gandhi once called “the eternal, involuntary fast.”

A recent survey by the United Nations Food and Agriculture Organization has shown anywhere from one-third to one-half of the world goes to bed hungry every night, and every day approximately ten thousand people die of starvation or diseases from malnourishment. In addition, every half minute, of one hundred children born in developing countries; twenty will die within the year, and sixty will suffer from malnutrition during the weaning and toddler stage with the possibility of irreversible physical and mental damage.

But hunger is more than cold facts and statistics; every number has a face. It is the face of a little boy in a refugee camp on the outskirts of Phnom Penh with swollen stomach, puffy face, and scaly skin. It is the face of a nomad who sits outside a camp of goatskin tents, once proud and independent, now waiting for the daily distribution of his handful of grain. It is the wrinkled, brown face of a mother who lives high in the mountains of Afghanistan, holding at her breast her baby who is in the last stages of malnourishment.

We hear the facts; we imagine the faces; but do we know the need? Most of us are like the Calcutta business man who after taking a visitor to see the work of Mother Theresa, was asked by his guest, “Where do all these people go in the winter?” He hesitated a moment and then replied, “I don’t know. I never really thought about it.” Like him, most of us are too far removed from hunger to really think about it.

But even when we know the need and feel some compassion, what do we do? Beginning with the Levitical commands to feed the poor and continuing with the teachings of Christ, the Bible makes it clear that God calls us, not just to pray for the hungry, but to feed them. If we take this call seriously, several things follow – some things we are not to do; some things we must do.

First, the things not to do. We are not to feel guilty. Guilt is a poor substitute for moral action and never puts food in anyone’s mouth. Secondly, we are not to feel overwhelmed. When confronting the magnitude of the problem, it is easy to feel like a pea shooter against a tank. But while one drop of water may not add much to a gallon of water, a drop of blue dye can change the color and a drop of chlorine can remove the contaminants.

We may not change the world, but we will make a difference if we do what we can.

Thirdly, we are not called to mouth easy solutions or explanations. To suggest that solving the hunger problem is simply a matter of population control or a distribution problem that technology will solve, is not only to simplify the problem, but to pass it on to someone else, and ultimately is no more helpful than to blame the victims by calling them lazy and unwilling to work.

And lastly, we are not called to simple acts of charity – as important as these may be. Delivering food baskets at Thanksgiving and Christmas may salve our conscience, but it does little to alleviate hunger during the rest of the year. Furthermore, it is often seen as a gift from one who is "up" to one who is "down" and does little to invest the recipient with hope and dignity. In this regard, jobs are more important than food baskets for they help to create something food baskets can't – a productive human being. Helping the hungry may be more a matter of justice than charity.

If we want to reduce hunger in a lasting way, we must truly engage the problem. Compassion and a concern for justice come when we are engaged with the need. There are any number of ways this can happen - through study and reading, visiting local food banks, going on crop walks, fasting or living on a subsistence diet, organizing community forums dealing with hunger issues, working to pass legislation like preservation of our farmland, and contributing to organizations like Bread for the World and the Heifer Project are all ways we can become more informed, help raise the consciousness of others, and make our own contribution. Whatever we do, however, it is important to avoid a one-dimensional approach since helping to alleviate hunger is not just a matter of doing one thing. Increasing our agricultural productivity, limiting our population, altering our lifestyle to exercise more fiscal restraint, sending food packages and financial support, and passing new laws are all needed. Finding an answer to hunger involves using every avenue available without pointing any fingers of blame. Charity and justice are both required.

Two things we can all do involve working to change our lifestyle and becoming more informed and active in regard to public policy issues. In both of these matters, Paul's letter to the early Christian community in Corinth reminds us we are to act with need and equality in mind; our giving should be, not so much out of our surplus, as out of a desire to create a more fair balance of the world's resources. We Americans who live on a livestock-based diet, not only use enough food to feed five Chinese, but use one-half of our agricultural land to feed animals. Since it takes ten to twenty pounds of grain to produce a pound of beef, it is understandable why the hungry might place a higher priority on using that grain to feed people instead of cattle, especially when decreasing our meat consumption by ten per cent would release enough grain to feed sixty million people. Knowing we consume sixty per cent of the world's resources while making up only six per cent of its population, it may be helpful to ask what determines our needs – how much are they governed by advertising, or culture and television? How much by the needs of the hungry? Is it possible to change from a product-consumption orientation to a more person-need orientation?

But addressing the hunger problem is not just a matter of producing more food for people; it is basically a question of who controls the production. One example is the Corn Products Corporation, which has introduced a new hybrid corn in Pakistan, but uses it, not to feed Pakistanis, but to produce corn sweetner for soft drinks in the U.S. A similar thing happens in South America where American business interests buy up land and use it, not to grow food for the local population, but to grow coffee that is shipped back to the states. Agricultural land is being taken out of production at a net rate of over a million acres a year. Suburban developers and corporations decide how the land is used, primarily on the basis of profit and convenience, not the needs of the world's hungry.

If Christ is to be the bread of life to the hungry, then we must seek to change public policy so we are helping people not only eat, but become educated and trained to feed themselves. To do this will involve both changes in our life style and public policy, but perhaps most of all – changes in our compassion and concern for justice. May we see the need and hear Christ's call that the hungry may indeed be fed.

"Not For Just a Day, But For a Lifetime"

There's a Chinese proverb that says, "Unless we change direction, we are likely to end up where we are headed." This warning seems particularly appropriate when it comes to the environment where we annually celebrate Earth Day and remind ourselves we have a problem, and then the rest of the year, revert to living as though the problem is not serious.

Each Earth Day we are made aware our water is increasingly unsafe to drink, our air quality is decreasing, the ozone continues to be depleted, the rain forests are vanishing, there are new "dead" zones in the ocean, the ice caps are melting, and several more animal species are becoming extinct. We then wave the green flag of Earth Day, blame corporations or the government for their indifference, recite the "technology will save us" mantra, and continue to view progress in primarily economic terms, all the while discounting the environmentalists as simply over-reacting.

As people called to be faithful stewards of creation, how can we change our response so it moves from an event-centered, temporary concern to a more, year-round, everyday lifestyle? While many suggestions are being made as to how this might be achieved, it seems to me the thing most needed is to adopt a less self-centered perspective; a perspective that transcends narrow self-interest and sees the world, not simply in terms of what benefits us, but what best serves the interest of planet earth.

Theologically, as the Psalmist reminds us, "The earth is the Lord's and all that is in it; the world and those who dwell therein." Put simply, the earth is not ours, but our Creator's. God has not set us here to subdue the earth, but to preserve it. We are to be stewards whose survival on this planet is not just a personal matter for me having enough; it is a matter of remembering with Chief Seattle, "We did not weave the web of life; we are merely strands in it. Whatever we do to the web, we do to ourselves." And ultimately our actions include our children as well as ourselves. Though we like to think what we have on this earth is ours alone, we might benefit from seeing things in the perspective of the Kenyan proverb, "The earth we inhabit is not a gift from our parents, but a loan from our children." We are called to be good stewards, not only on God's behalf, but also for the sake of those who come after us.

If we forget our interdependence, if we compete instead of cooperate, if we seek to subdue instead of preserve, we may become the agents of our own destruction. We need to move beyond a "we" verses "they" mentality that pits developing nations against the developed, capitalists against socialists, environmentalists against corporations, and individuals against the government. Whenever we fail to put aside these divisions, the so called "*enemy*" is not "*them*", but "*us*". We need to view the world in terms of unities, not units; not compartments, but interdependence. Instead of crying out, "NIMBY" (not in my backyard), we ought to shorten it to NOPE (not on planet earth). If it's not acceptable to me, why should it be acceptable to someone else?

The importance of transcending narrow self-interest is wonderfully told in one of Anthony de Mello's parables. Annoyed with the stomach, other parts of the body resent that they have to procure food and bring it to the stomach while the stomach itself does nothing but devour the fruit of their labor. So they decide they will no longer bring the stomach food. The hands will no longer lift it to the mouth. The teeth will not chew it. The throat will not swallow it. In this way, they will force the stomach to do something. But all they succeed in doing is to make the body weak to the point that they are all threatened with death. At this point they realize, in helping one another, they are really working for their own welfare.

Seeing the big picture and giving up our need to always be in control may mean learning to accept the inevitable cycles of green and dry, birth and death, cold and warm, emptiness and fullness, light and dark; it may mean learning to be content with life's ebb and flow. As Anne Lindberg writes in Gift From the Sea, "We have little faith in the ebb and flow of life. We leap at the flow of the tide and resist in terror its ebb, afraid it will never return. We insist on permanency, on duration, on continuity when the only continuity possible is in growth and fluidity.

We resist aging and spend billions of dollars on cosmetic surgery and hair colorings and treatments to make us look young. We strive to extend the shelf life of perishable foods and spend billions more on packaging and preservatives, filling our landfills and adding unnecessary chemicals to our diet. We resist death and go to great lengths and expense to make the dead look like they are still alive. We live in a society that is ever-restless, always eager for more mountains to climb, seeking happiness through more and more possessions. As children of this culture we are seldom at peace with what we have. Can we learn with the apostle Paul to be content with whatever we have, knowing it is enough, and trusting our striving can cease in the abundance of God's grace? Can we become like the poet's "last" leaf, "One leaf left on a branch, and not a sound of sadness. All by itself, yet it does not speak of loneliness or death. One leaf and it spends itself swaying mildly in the breeze."

Practicing restraint and learning to be satisfied with what we have is a hard thing to learn. If one is good, two seems better so we are encouraged to buy one and get the second at half price even when we only need one. As a result, most families have at least two cars, two televisions, and three or four phones. Like our teens, we often get caught up in labels, brand names, and what our peers have. Learning to share, borrow, or rent goes against the grain of our culture's individualism and its emphasis on independence. The thought of doing without is scarcely entertained. But from an environmental standpoint, sustainability is more important than expediency and efficiency, and giving up convenience and comfort is sometimes needed for us to be environmentally responsible.

If this beautiful planet we inhabit is to be truly nurtured by us, we need to see our care for it extends beyond a special day to our entire lifetime. Making this change will not only improve the place where we reside, but ourselves as well. Essentially, Earth Day and its reminder to preserve the earth, has to do with our relationships and the oneness of all life. It is moving beyond narrow self-interest and seeing the big picture, remembering we are but tiny blossoms on the tree of life. It is giving up our need to always be in control, realizing the earth does not belong to us; we belong to it.

Sometimes we are tempted to lose ourselves in action, and action is important. But maybe it's time we become gardeners of the Spirit. Gardeners who sit under a tree, not with a book, or a companion, but alone where we observe the falling of a leaf, hear the lapping of the water, watch the flight of a bird. Then, perhaps, we shall truly appreciate the beauty of nature, but even more, experience a breakthrough to another world… for beyond the leaf, the water, and the bird lies the great darkness of the ultimate Dreamer – the one who dreamed our existence.

"God and the Space Age"

Today as we and millions like us sit before our television sets, we will be witnessing what many are calling the most historic event since we humans first inhabited the planet earth – two men will step down on the lunar surface 250,000 miles away from where their journey began. As William Prochnau, the New York Times staff reporter, has put it, "Science fiction has become science now, and flamboyant imagination *is* reality."

In one way, this moon visit marks the culmination of human dreams, but in another way, it is only the beginning. Unlike those who have climbed Mt. Everest, the world's highest mountain, the astronauts have only touched down on the first phase of humanity's journey to the stars – other, more-distant planetary bodies remain. And for many members of the scientific community this all seems to be a natural, even if difficult, first step in exploring the universe. Given sufficient time and resources, many feel that our technological knowledge will carry us far beyond the moon.

With these kinds of possibilities for extending our human frontiers, some very important questions need to be raised. Could the 25 billion dollars spent on this manned-space program be put to better use, especially were it directed toward solving the problems of race, poverty, and pollution? And more philosophically, how much should the future be shaped by what is technically possible verses what is humanly useful? And perhaps, most basic of all, who shall make this decision?

While the church should never hesitate to raise these kinds of questions, we should be careful about how we do it. There is no need to apologize for raising the question of human usefulness, but neither is there any reason to do so in an antagonistic manner. Too many times in the church's past it has challenged scientific knowledge at the wrong point. Galileo was forced by a church inquisition to give up his belief that the sun is the central body around which the earth and planets revolve, and the church denounced Darwin for his theory of evolution, claiming it contradicted the Biblical account of creation.

Today we need to realize that the clash between science and religion is ill-founded. When we say that the truth of the Biblical account of creation must be accepted literally or not at all, we pose an unreal problem, making the Bible become something it was never intended to be – a science, text book. We should never make the Bible's validity dependent upon its world-view – a child-like view when it comes to science because it sees the world without benefit of any scientific instruments. And besides, the Bible asks a totally different question than science – it asks "why"?, not "how"?

Given their understanding of the world, the writers of Genesis were more poetic than scientific in their view of life. The claim that the Bible is witness to God's word by no means involves the assertion that all its particular statements are infallible. Assembled over a period of more than a thousand years, it is not surprising that there are two different Biblical accounts of creation and the understanding of God is an evolving one. Scripture shares in the human nature into which it came, and as a result, it is recorded by men whose world-view is conditioned by their historic time, not ours.

It is important to clarify that the picture of the world presented in the Bible is only the language in which the word of God is spoken. Just as it makes no difference to the meaning of the word "*man*" whether it is spoken in Greek or German or English, so it makes absolutely no difference whether the story of God as creator is told in the language of the ancient church or the modern scientific view of the world. As the apostle Paul warned, "The letter kills, but the spirit gives life." A rigid holding to the *"letter"* in understanding the Bible has driven many people into a false choice – a choice in which there is a conflict between faith and honesty. The church's task is not to fight against science, but to be an agent of Christ's love, bringing healing and reconciliation to the world.

To speak to people today the church needs a radical openness to the future – the kind of openness displayed by Jesus when confronted by the Syrophoenician woman. When approached by this woman's request to cure her daughter, Jesus tells her, "Let the children first be fed, for it is not right to take the children's bread and throw it to the dogs." In this not so subtle way, Jesus reveals a narrow-minded bias, telling her that she and her race are not nearly as important to him as the Jews; in his mind, his mission to the Jews does not include Gentiles. But when the woman persists with her request, reminding him that even the dogs under the table are given crumbs to eat, Jesus has a change of heart. Where he has been close-minded and tied to his Jewish background, he now decides his ministry cannot be for the Jews alone, but must expand to include the Gentiles. What at first appeared to be an impossible request now becomes a very radical "*yes*", confirming John's gospel when it says, "Jesus grew in wisdom and stature."

It is this kind of openness that we in the church need to exercise toward the world today. Instead of being threatened and retreating to the security of yesterday's answers, we need to be open to the future. Instead of fearing what scientific knowledge may bring, we need to make certain it brings a more human world. As Wernher Von Braun, the man who heads the team of scientists that developed the engines powering the Apollo flight has said, "We need a greater Lord than we have had in the past. Our religion, our environment and our outlook have been earthbound. We must learn to consider God as creator of the universe and master of everything, not just the earth."

Our flight to the moon signals the dawn of a new age in which the earth will be seen as a planet among planets, and in which the magnificence of divine creation and power will become increasingly evident. Yet, it is an age that will not escape its problems on earth simply by going to the moon. While eyes all over the world will be focused on astronauts Amstrong, Aldrin, and Collins, those same eyes belong to people caught up in all the pain and suffering of the world - eyes of Senators arguing whether to ring the U.S. with a nuclear shield; eyes of a husband and wife not getting along; eyes of the old, feeling they are no longer needed; eyes of the young, wanting to give themselves to a great cause, but not knowing what; eyes of the poor, wondering why they've been left out; and eyes of Biafrans and Vietnamese, longing for peace.

Will these eyes continue to be filled with worry and longing, or will they begin to know a sense of peace? There can be no simple answer, but a series of murals in the entrance of Radio City in New York city suggests a helpful picture. The first three murals show humanity's progress. The fourth shows Jesus on the side of a hill surrounded by a mass of people. Underneath are the words, "Man's ultimate destiny depends not on whether he can learn new lessons or make new discoveries, but on his acceptance of the lesson taught him 2,000 years ago." If we are to not only survive, but continue to celebrate our scientific and technological skills, we must learn to live together in love, making certain our scientific breakthroughs lead to a more compassionate and just world.

"Interpreting the Signs of the Times"

In Luke's gospel, Jesus addresses the crowd with a question, "When you see a cloud looming in the west you say at once that rain is coming, and so it does. And when the wind is from the south you say it's going to be hot, and so it is. You know how to interpret the face of the earth and sky. How is it you do not know how to interpret these times?" In other words, Jesus asks, "If we can predict the weather, why are we so blind to the social and political events of our day*?"*

Gordon Hinckley, president of Iliff Seminary, suggests that interpreting the signs of the times is one of the primary ministries of today's church. In his recent book, Images of Ministry, he claims, "It is imperative that churches help people see the world they live in with the eyes of faith." What might it mean for us to do that today?

Numerous futurists have written about the trends of our contemporary world. One of the main trends mentioned is the shift from the atom to the bit, or as others have named it – the move from the industrial society to the information society. Without pretending to be comprehensive, let me point to some interesting aspects of this shift.

We marvel at the benefits technology brings to our lives, making things more convenient and giving us access to information our grandparents never dreamed possible. To access the weather in distant places, to call a friend while driving in a car, to pay bills on-line, and to immediately find answers to historical questions and learn about any topic imaginable without leaving home are all wonderful products of today's technology. But like most things, these marvels do not come without a cost – a cost that is not simply monetary, and should not be taken lightly.

The first cost that I'll mention is the accelerated pace of life. While technology has brought convenience to modern life, it has also quickened our pace. As a society geared toward quick fixes, we have frequently speeded up our eating habits with television dinners in the microwave and take-away meals at fast-food stops – neither of which is conducive to either a healthy diet or sitting down for a family meal.

Similarly, our communication patterns have been speeded up with e-mails filling our computer in-boxes; call-waiting making certain we don't miss anyone; pagers keeping us continuously available; and cell phones insuring we have no "dead" time from work. The result is often information over-load and increased stress. Some people, including my wife, Pat, are deciding to reduce their use of e-mail because the more often it is sent, the more one gets back, and the more difficult it is to keep up. Instead of reducing our work load, the ease with which e-mail and cell phones enable us to keep in touch may actually be increasing both our work load and our level of stress.

Perhaps, it is time to ask ourselves if living faster is also healthier. Do more information and an accelerated pace of life necessarily lead to better decisions? Is it not important to build some Sabbath time into our busy schedules – time when we are not just "*getting away*" or "*eating on the run*", but taking time for reflection and meditation, for prayer and family conversation? The rush to buy the latest technological gadget may make our life more exciting, but does it mean there should be no evaluation or discernment process before "*buying in*"? Where do we draw the line on what is useful?

A second area where the benefits of technology need to be weighed against the cost is the effect it has on our personal relationships. While the internet has given us access to people around the world, it does not necessarily mean we have deepened our personal relationships. As Theodore Reiseman's The Lonely Crowd points out, "We can talk with people all over the world, but may not really know our neighbors." While the use of the internet has broadened our personal contacts and re-defined who is a stranger, it has also increased parental worries when teenagers use the internet to make friends with people whom they've never met in person. What guidelines does a parent use to draw the line in this regard? With sexual predators taking advantage of unsuspecting, lonely, troubled teens many parents have begun setting limits and safeguards on the use of their computers, recognizing that issues of trust and privacy are not as easily safeguarded when there is no eye-to-eye contact.

Another challenging aspect of living in this information society is the constant stimulation that surrounds us. Where people used to take walks simply to exercise and enjoy their natural surroundings, now walkers and joggers are often accompanied by a walkman or an I-pod headset. While there is nothing wrong with having music as a companion, I wonder if we have lost our capacity to be alone and the time for reflection solitude affords. The prevalence of loud music and widespread use of cell phones in public places seems omnipresent; neither camping out in the woods nor eating in a restaurant guarantee we will be surrounded by peace and quiet when someone at the next table or campsite starts talking on their cell phone or playing their boom box.

As television and the internet increasingly replace newspapers as our primary information source, our news tends to come in sound bites and focus on the sensational. Not surprisingly, the local news often resembles a police blotter. A child falling into a well can dominate the news for days. In the top box-office movies character development and story line have given way to action-packed thrillers with lots of shoot-em-up, chase scenes. It's no wonder many suffer from attention deficit disorder and the sale of drugs like Ritalin are booming, especially among children who have been raised on television cartoons and video games and seem to need constant stimulation.

As a result of this constant stimulation, it seems it is more difficult for people to entertain themselves. When children aren't able to watch television or play with their computers, boredom often results. The more television serves as a baby sitter, the more children seem to complain about having nothing to do when the television goes on the blink. Spending more time watching television and playing video games has led to what some have called "*spectatoritis*" – the condition that arises when we are more often spectators than participants. Where this happens, not only is there a decline in physical activity, there is often a corresponding rise in obesity. We are increasingly a nation that is physically less fit, often overweight, and suffering from diabetes and related health issues.

Obviously, it is unfair to place the blame for our accelerated pace of life and the decline in our physical fitness and health entirely at the hands of technology. But while we should not make technology the scapegoat for these things, neither should we ignore the challenges it presents. As people of faith, we need to continually ask and seek to understand both the benefits and costs these technological advances present. Ultimately, the most important question in discerning the changes initiated by our move into the information age will always be, "Will technology be our slave or our master?" If it becomes the latter, we may lose, not only our freedom, but the place we have been given as stewards of God's creation.

Part III - Introducing Jesus

"The central issue of the Christian life is not believing in God or the Bible, but entering into a relationship with the risen, living Christ." Marcus Borg

Some forty years ago, when I was in seminary, I took a course in Christology. In the course we studied about the historical Jesus and how theologians, both ancient and contemporary, understood him. We delved into such things as the virgin birth, his divine and human nature, his death and resurrection. It was an exciting time, but the most memorable day of the class came when our professor, in the midst of quizzing us as to who certain theologians claimed Christ to be, suddenly stopped and turning to me, asked, "What about you, Mr. Smith? Who do you say Christ is?"

I don't remember what I said then, but it's a question I've thought about many times since. Sometimes it has come up in regard to a particular Biblical text, like the one in Matthew where Jesus asks Peter, "Who do you say that I am?" Sometimes it has arisen when teaching a class dealing with images of Christ such as "Savior" and "Redeemer," and sometimes it has occurred as I've struggled to understand and clarify the church's mission.

It is a question that has elicited a variety of responses throughout history. Even in Jesus' time, people weren't sure who he was. Some considered him to be one of the prophets, while others thought he was the reincarnation of John the Baptist. To some he was the Son of the Living God, but others claimed he was simply a lawbreaker who thumbed his nose at religious authority.

When people are asked who Jesus is today, conflicting opinions still continue. For some he is the Alpha and Omega, the beginning and end whom they know as their Lord and Savior; but for others he is merely a noble example - a good man upon whom the church has bestowed an exalted status.

The sermons that follow attempt to aid the reader in wrestling with this question of Jesus' identity. Jesus is seen in the various roles he played and the way his life was lived on the stage of history – first, in the way he carried out his ministry as teacher and story-teller, healer and miracle-worker; and second, through sermons dealing with the Christmas and Easter stories.

Looking at Jesus as "teacher" and "story-teller," we can see by the subjects he addressed what things were important to him and gain an even deeper appreciation of what he valued and how he looked at the world. Seeing Jesus as "healer" shows, not only the depth of his compassion, but even more its breadth. Those whose health he restored included the blind, the lame, the deaf, and the mentally disturbed. While many of these healings appear miraculous, Jesus' view of miracles is not what one might think.

Looking at Jesus through the lens of Christmas and Easter provides an opportunity to see him in yet a different light. May each of these sermons bring enlightenment and encouragement to strengthen and inspire our daily life.

Jesus: The Teacher

"I am indebted to my father for living, but to my teacher for living well." Alexander of Macedon

Teaching was a central part of Jesus' ministry. It began at the age of twelve when his parents found him in the temple, sitting among the teachers of the Law, engaging them in dialogue, and asking questions that astounded all who heard him. His teaching was not, however, confined to a certain period, as it lasted throughout his life.

Jesus' teaching was spontaneous; neither confined to the temple nor any formal setting. Other than the time he addressed the crowds with the Sermon on the Mount, his teaching was primarily done through everyday conversations with people. Sometimes he taught by commenting on what he observed; sometimes by questioning the actions of others; and sometimes in response to questions he was asked. Other times, like when he rode the donkey into Jerusalem during the Passover and when he was arrested and crucified, he taught by the example of his actions.

Much of his teaching evoked strong reaction as it often required more than the Judaic law, focusing on the spirit behind the law more than its letter. Hence, while Judaic law prohibited murder and adultery, Jesus said one should not even be angry with another or have a lustful heart. While the law taught an eye for an eye and a tooth for a tooth, Jesus said one should pray for his enemy and turn the other cheek. Where the law proscribed correct behavior, Jesus wanted not only good behavior, but also a positive and compassionate attitude.

The central theme of Jesus' teaching could be summed up in one sentence - seek first the kingdom of God. If one puts God first, Jesus says everything else will take care of itself. For Jesus, all the commandments of the law centered around two things: loving God and loving one's neighbor. As he told the young lawyer who asked what one must do to gain eternal life, doing these two things was all that was needed.

In looking at the teachings of Jesus, I have chosen four sermons that relate to the things Jesus cared most about: his relationship with God, determining "right" from "wrong", and one's relationships with others, as affected, first, by one's judgments, and secondly, by one's capacity to forgive. What he says about each of these will provide a clearer insight into Jesus' mind and his understanding of the things he values.

What Jesus Taught About God

Seeing her little four-year-old's drawing, the mother asks her daughter what it is. "I'm drawing a picture of God," is the surprising reply. "But," her mother responds, "no one knows what God looks like." Looking up briefly, the child sweetly replies, "Well, they will when I'm done."

Her claim is one Jesus might also have made. His picture, however, is not an artistic creation, but rather is revealed through stories and every day conversation. Though rooted in his Judaic upbringing, Jesus' picture of God enlarges Judaism's emphasis. Where Israel's God looked primarily at the well being of the Jews, the God whom Jesus pictures has a more universal concern and presence.

Even though Psalm 139 says God's presence is everywhere, "If I scale the heavens you are there, if I make my bed in hell, you are there. If I fly away on the wings of the dawn or dwell beyond the ocean, even there your hand will guide me," another strain in Judaism sees God as belonging to our country, but not our enemies. God is on our side, but not the side of others. Freeing the Israelites from their Egyptian slavery, God visited the Egyptians with plagues and killed their first born.

Jesus, however, speaks of God as one whose compassion transcends national boundaries. In his sermon on the mount, Jesus points out that God "causes the sun to rise on the bad as well as the good, and sends rain to fall on the upright and wicked alike." When an earnest, young lawyer asks Jesus, "Who is my neighbor?" *Jesus* tells the story of the good Samaritan, using a foreigner as the one who demonstrates God-like love as he comes to the aid of the victim. When Jesus talks about God, his emphasis is on a God who is everywhere, transcending national boundaries and universally present.

In addition to seeing God's love is for all, Jesus teaches that God is <u>directly accessible</u>. Many primitive religions saw God only through intermediaries. Moses could not look directly upon God, but saw him through a burning bush. To the prophets, God spoke through angels. Only the priests could enter the holy of holies, the most sacred part of the temple where God was believed to reside; the common people could only come to God through the mediation of the priests.

When Jesus discusses prayer, he says no intermediaries are needed; there is a direct line of communication with God for every person. "When you pray," he says, "go into your private room and God who sees in secret will reward you openly." Jesus mentioned going into your private room, not as a necessity to contact the divine, but only to point out that we are not to make a show of our religion like the Pharisees who love to pray openly on the street corner so their devotion to God may be known by others.

One place where Jesus is most at odds with his Jewish heritage is its reliance on the law. For the Israel of Jesus' day, good works, often defined as keeping the law, became a wall between God and the people. Law, in becoming man's real authority, no longer leads to meeting with God, but rather leads either to pride of accomplishment or guilt at failure to obey it. In contrast, Jesus seeks to liberate the will of God from its petrifaction in tablets of stone and reaches for the heart of man which seeks seclusion and safety behind the observance of the law. This difference is seen most clearly when Jesus tells the story of the Pharisee and the Publican.

When the two men went up to the temple to pray, the Pharisee thanked God that he was not grasping, unjust, and adulterous like everyone else, and particularly not like the tax collector who stood beside him. The tax collector simply asks God for mercy. In commenting on the story, Jesus emphasizes that God is less impressed by our pride in keeping the religious law than in our humility - something characterized by the tax collector's plea, "God be merciful to me, a sinner."

Another emphasis in Jesus' portrayal of God is on God's sense of justice. While the Old Testament prophets called for justice, they also exhibited a readiness to bargain with God. Gideon used the fleece-test, first requiring the fleece be wet with dew and the ground around it dry and then the reverse, before accepting God's call to lead the Israelites into battle. Abraham bargained with God to save the city of Sodom, reducing the number of righteous needed to save the city from fifty men to ten.

In contrast, Jesus says God is unalterably opposed to evil, and he does not compromise with it. In several stories, he makes it clear that not everyone who calls upon God for mercy will be saved. The one-talent man who buries his talent is cast into the darkness of hell. The wedding attendants who couldn't greet the bridegroom because they failed to keep enough oil to keep their lamps burning, were not allowed entrance into the wedding hall. Those who excuse themselves from the banquet shall not ever taste the feast they miss out on. Jesus makes it clear that not everyone who calls out "Lord, Lord" will be saved.

Yet, the God of justice is also a God of mercy who reaches out to us. Nowhere is this more clearly seen than in the story Jesus tells of the prodigal son. After wasting his father's inheritance, the son returns home hungry and out of work, and like a dog with its tail between its legs, asks only to be taken on as a servant in his father's household. But to his surprise, even before he can make his confession and ask for mercy, his father runs to meet him on his return home, throws his arms around him, kisses him, and orders the servants to bring clothes and sandals, put a ring around his finger, and kill the fatted calf to celebrate his return. While our failures to honor God are never to be excused as of no consequence, the God whom Jesus portrays is always waiting for us at the end of the road.

A story is told about a missionary who was sent to a jungle land where the inhabitants had practiced cannibalism, and still maintained the custom of taking the head of a person once a year, during a special feast day. The missionary, who had tried for years to get them to end the practice, finally convinced them to take the head of whoever should walk down a certain path at the break of dawn on the day of the annual feast. After some discussion, they agreed and on the morning of the appointed day, stood waiting by the side of the path when approaching footsteps were heard. Unable to see clearly in the pre-dawn hour, they let fly with their spears. But when they ran forward to claim their victim, they were shocked to discover it was the missionary. It was a crazy, stupid thing for the missionary to do, but it did end their head-hunting.

It's this kind of self-giving love that God has for us. When we look at the cross, we are reminded that there is one who reaches out to us, begging that we leave our blind prejudices and end our hurtful behaviors. For as Jesus paints the picture of God, it is of one who unalterably opposes evil, yet extends mercy beyond our wildest imagination; a God who is everywhere present, directly accessible, waiting for us to reciprocate his love.

What Jesus Teaches About Right and Wrong

For people of Jesus' day the key factor in determining "right" from "wrong" was determined by the question, "Is it within the Law?" Does it uphold the Ten Commandments that Moses passed down from Mt. Sinai? Is it faithful to the dietary and other requirements of the Levitical code? For the Israelites, these are the important questions in determining "right" and "wrong". But for Jesus, these questions are not enough; determining "right" and "wrong" requires something more, and insisting there must be something more is where Jesus runs into trouble with the religious authorities who are the Law's "gate-keepers".

This "more" for Jesus involves several things, all of which make the point that upholding the spirit of the Law is more important than merely fulfilling the letter of the Law. One can dutifully fulfill the letter of the law by strictly following the dietary restrictions the law dictates and ignore the beggar at one's door. And a person may attend all the religious festivals and tithe one's earnings, and still forget about the needs of the poor and the sick.

Jesus does not upset the religious leaders of his day, challenging their understanding of "right and wrong" by criticizing certain inadequacies of the Law and insisting they be changed; his objections are not to the Law per se, but rather to their interpretation and use of it. In fact, he is a strong supporter of the Law, insisting he has not come to abolish the Law or the Prophets, but to complete them. When he says, "In truth I tell you, till heaven and earth disappear, not one dot, not one little stroke, is to disappear from the Law until all its purposes are achieved," it is clear he supports the Law. And when he adds, "Anyone who infringes even one of the least of these commandments and teaches others to do the same will be considered least in the kingdom of Heaven," there is no doubt his regard for the Law is of the highest order.

But when it comes to determining "right" from "wrong", despite his high regard for the Law, there are at least three ways Jesus feels the Law is inadequate: (1) it provides an external rather than internal standard; (2) its emphasis is not positive and active enough; and (3) it holds itself above human need. Let us now turn to each of these in order.

For Jesus, righteousness is a matter of the heart as well as the deed. Upholding the Law may satisfy the religious authorities, but in Jesus' eyes outward conformity is not enough. He sets a higher standard, contrasting the requirements of the Law with his own thoughts and teaching. Where ancestral teaching says do not commit murder, he says anyone who is angry with a brother, anyone who calls another "fool" will answer for it in hell;

where the Law says do not commit adultery, he says if a man looks at a woman lustfully, he has already committed adultery with her in his heart; where the Law says anyone who divorces his wife must give her a writ of divorce, Jesus says anyone who divorces his wife, except for the case of an illicit marriage, makes her an adulteress; and when the Law says you must not break your oath, he says do not swear at all…all you need say is 'yes' and 'no'. And most challenging of all, Jesus says that instead of an eye for an eye and a tooth for tooth response to an enemy, one must love his enemy, turning his cheek and praying for his persecutor.

In Jesus' eyes the Law falls short because it provides an external rather than an internal standard; it focuses primarily on what one does, but Jesus includes one's thoughts and attitudes as well. Goodness is not determined by one's outward appearance as much as by what is in one's heart. Hence, the poor widow who places two small coins in the treasury is praised more than those who have given much larger amounts because she has given all she has while they have only given out of their surplus, and to make a show of their generosity.

A second place where Jesus challenges the Law is his claim that it is not positive and active enough; for Jesus, passive morality is not to be praised. His blessing is for the peacemakers, not the peace keepers. People can love peace and declare they are in favor of it, yet do nothing to advance its cause. One can say he is for treating all people equally, yet refuse to rent to someone whose skin is a different color or whose sexual bias is different from his own.

For Jesus, the ultimate test in receiving God's final blessing depends upon a series of active verbs – feeding the hungry, providing water for the thirsty, clothing the naked, visiting the sick and imprisoned, and welcoming the stranger. When Jesus tells the story of the Good Samaritan it is worth noting that the priest and the Levite broke no moral law; they merely passed by on the other side. The good Samaritan who comes to the aid of the man who has been beaten and robbed, on the other hand, actively ministers to him, cleaning and disinfecting his wounds, bandaging them, taking him to an inn to recover, and telling the innkeeper he will cover any expenses related to the man's recovery. While he doesn't explicitly say so, it is obvious Jesus considers sins of omission to be just as bad as sins of commission. Doing the "right" thing for Jesus is not just a matter of staying out of trouble; it also entails confronting trouble and seeking to overcome it.

Perhaps, what Jesus finds most disturbing about using the Law as a moral guide is that it too often puts obedience to the Law above human need. For this reason, he is critical of those who condemn his treating the sick on the Sabbath. When they complain his acts of healing violate the Sabbath commandment to honor the day by abstaining from any physical activity, he reminds them that the Sabbath was made for man, and not man for the Sabbath. For Jesus, the key question is always whether the deed meets some human need.

Jesus says all the commandments can be summed up by two things: love God with all your heart, soul, mind, and strength, and secondly, love your neighbor as yourself. The essence of goodness is love, and the kind of love Jesus has in mind needs no list of rules – it creates its own program of goodness. For Jesus, the whole law is fulfilled in this one little word – love.

If we are to follow the example and teachings of Jesus in determining "right" from "wrong", what, then, are we to do? First, and foremost, we must first ask, "What is the course of action which love dictates?" And then, we must strive to make sure our response is rooted in compassion and positive action that puts human need first. If we do this, not so others will applaud our actions, but simply to please God, we can be sure we are following the road that Jesus would have us walk.

What Jesus Says About Judging Others

The sound bites of judgment surround us. "That was a terrible performance!" "That kid shouldn't be playing – he never listens." " Look how messy their yard is." "She's too slow to be a cashier." " She has the worst voice in the choir." " Can you believe how low she wears her pants! "

And sometimes the judgments are not just comments others make, but things we say ourselves. We judge the speech, the dress, the looks, and the performance of people constantly. Yet, Jesus says we should not judge. As Matthew records it, Jesus makes it clear we shall be judged as we judge others, "Do not judge, and you will not be judged for as you judge others, you will be judged. First, take the log out of your own eye then you will see clearly to take the splinter out of your brother's eye."

Obviously, Jesus does not mean by this that we are to avoid moral discrimination. Should we overlook such things as lying, cheating, stealing, or playing the hypocrite on grounds we should not judge our fellow man? Absolutely not! Jesus takes it for granted it is necessary to make judgments. He warns his followers to beware of wolves in sheep's clothing. He says a tree should be known by the fruit it bears. He himself is in constant judgment on those who scrupulously wash the outside of the cup, but leave the inside dirty. And he reprimands those who seek places of prominence, saying the first shall be last and the last first.

The key to understanding how Jesus differentiates between judging that is appropriate and judging that is not, is found both in the situation being judged, and also in the attitude of the one doing the judging. When people's lives are being hurt, remaining silent is not appropriate. Hence, Jesus condemns those who hide behind a religious law rather than help someone in need. But while Jesus acknowledges any failure to help one who suffers needs to be called into question, there is no place for self-righteous judging. When a woman anoints Jesus with an expensive ointment, his disciples complain about the waste, saying it can be better spent on the poor. But Jesus comes to the woman's defense, seeing the anointing as an act of devotion and asking the disciples why they are upsetting the woman with their complaints.

While it is relatively easy to identify and make judgments about those places where society falls short - not providing adequate, low-cost child care for working mothers, insurance and lending practices that discriminate against minorities, and insufficient low-cost housing to name a few, it is not as easy to avoid blaming others while being blind to our own responsibility.

If we are to avoid the self-righteous judging Jesus abhors, it is important we look at ourselves before judging others. Whereas genuine concern is illuminating, judging others makes us blind. The story of David in the Old Testament is an excellent example of how judging others can lead to our own blindness. When the prophet Nathan tells David about the rich man who has taken the poor man's lamb, David's anger blazes at the injustice. The very thought that a man who has thousands of sheep should kill his poor neighbor's only lamb in order to feed a stranger causes David to call for the rich man's death. In David's eyes the poor man should be repaid four times over. But then, just when he has pronounced his judgment, Nathan tells David, "You are the man," suggesting he look in the mirror before voicing his wrath.

When we assume the role of judge we are not thereby exempt from judgment ourselves. In judging others it is all too easy to blind ourselves to our own evil and ignore the grace others are just as entitled to as we are. There's a rather humorous story about a family criticizing the church service they've just attended. The father notes that the sermon was lousy; the mother says the choir sang poorly; and the sister chimes in that the organist played too loud. Whereupon the ten-year old son quips, "Yeh, but it wasn't a bad show for a quarter." As someone has said, "The faults you see in others, take care to shun. If you'll only look at home there's enough to be done."

A second aid in reigning in our tendency to justify ourselves by judging others is to look at others from within. How much better off might we be if we took seriously the Indian proverb, "Don't judge a man until you've walked two months in his moccasins." If our judgments are grounded in genuine concern for another, we cannot look at others with detachment for to do so is to hold them at arm's length and not get close to them; it is to pin a label on them, and not see them growing. As Clarence Jordan, who founded the inter-racial farm in Georgia, has written, "Jesus reminds us there is one judgment and one grace that ultimately matters – God's." Hence, we who would be Christ's disciple's will look upon others, not with a spirit of detachment, but as people like ourselves – forgiven sinners who owe their lives to the love of God.

Perhaps, the primary reason we are not to judge others is that we all stand exposed to God's judging, and we should not expect mercy from God if we are not ready to be merciful to our fellow brothers and sisters. Jesus reminds us all what it means to be merciful when he tells Peter the story about a king who decides to settle accounts with one of his workers. The man's debt has run into the thousands, and since he has no means of paying the debt, the master orders him to be sold along with his wife, children, and everything he owns. The servant falls at the master's feet and begs him to be patient, saying he will repay the debt in full if only given more time. The master is so moved with pity that he lets the man go and cancels his debt. But no sooner has the man gone out than he meets a fellow servant who owes him a few dollars. Grabbing hold of his fellow servant by the throat, he demands to be paid what he is owed. When the fellow servant begs him to be patient, saying he will repay the debt at a later time, the servant has him thrown in jail. When the king hears what has happened, he is so angry he condemns the man to torture. Jesus says that is how God will deal with us unless we forgive our brothers and sisters. It is primarily for our own good that Jesus warns us against harsh judging. Life gives back what we pour into it. Hate hurts the hater more than the hated; jealousy, greed, and pride do more damage to the personality of the person who harbors them than to the one against whom they are directed.

Jesus teaches that we are to be uncritical, but this does not mean we are to be neutral toward moral issues. We are not asked to overlook completely such things as lying, stealing, cheating, or playing the hypocrite. No one is asked to remain silent in the face of wrong. But we must be extremely careful when we engage in ethical appraisal that we do so in the spirit of Christ. It is not an approved standard of righteous behavior that alone guides our thought; it is also the knowledge that in our sister and brother we see one to whom Chris comes – one like us, who has similar shortcomings and a similar need for God's grace. May all persons we encounter see in us signs of God's grace, and may we leave the judgment of their worthiness to God.

Jesus Speaks of Forgiveness

The need for forgiveness is all around us – a driver passes in a no-passing zone and nearly runs us off the road, someone cuts in front of us as we stand in line at a movie, the next door apartment dweller plays his tv until after midnight, our spouse forgets our wedding anniversary, our ex-husband refuses to pay child support, a fellow worker takes credit for our work and gets the promotion we deserve. And we can all add to the list.

But as great as the need for forgiveness, the difficulty of practicing forgiveness is even greater. We'd like to think it's a quick, once-and-for-all event, but it is most often a slow, on-going process. Forgiveness may not be granted even when we plead for it on our knees, and when it's given, it may not be appreciated, and when it's unappreciated, it may be rescinded.

Is it any wonder why it's been said that the real test of Christian living comes when we've been wronged. Only then can the deepest, truest love be seen – love willing to forgive. As a minister friend of mine once said, "Nothing in this world bears the imprint of God so surely as forgiveness."

The importance of forgiveness, especially for those who would follow Christ, is underlined in scripture where it is a central theme. Joseph forgives his brothers who throw him into the pit and sell him into slavery. God forgives Nineveh, the city whose wickedness offends him. Jesus forgives the woman taken in adultery, and later explains God's forgiveness, telling a parable about a father who forgives his prodigal son after the son has squandered his inheritance. When Peter asks Jesus, "How many times must I forgive", he is told, "Not seven, but seventy times seven." And not surprisingly, the prayer Jesus teaches his disciples also emphasizes forgiveness, making it clear God's forgiveness is related to our forgiving others.

When Jesus speaks of forgiveness, he never fails to let people know that the future can overcome their past. Several pictures from his life show that Jesus gives all whom he meets a redemptive hope. Three pictures worth looking at are his words and actions when an adulteress is brought before him, his encounter with Zacchaeus, and the hope he imparts to others when he is hanging from the cross.

For the women caught in the act of adultery, her future is grim as the law of her day makes clear that punishment for her sin is death by stoning. She no doubt considers her self doomed – chained to her past. When the Pharisees who bring the women to Jesus ask him what he has to say,

Jesus bends down and starts writing on the ground with his finger. As they persist with their question, he straightens up and says, "Let the one among you who is guiltless be the first to throw a stone at her." With these words, Jesus puts the woman's sin in a different light, asking that those who condemn her see her sin in light of their own. When the crowd disperses, Jesus asks the woman, "Has not one condemned you?" and being told no one has, he adds, "Neither do I. Go and sin no more."

This picture of Jesus makes clear forgiveness can have a dramatic impact on a person's life, opening a door to the future that has been closed. But for this to happen, those who are her accusers are asked to see the sin of this woman whom they condemn in light of their own shortcomings. For Jesus, true forgiveness is grounded in the recognition of our own need for forgiveness.

Apart from the usual complaints that Jesus is associating with a sinner, his going to Zacchaeus' house for dinner seems rather tame in comparison to the story of Jesus and the adulteress woman, but the change in Zacchaeus is no less dramatic. During the meal, Zacchaeus, who is has become quite wealthy using his position as a hated tax collector to exploit people, announces to Jesus that he is going to give half of his property to the poor, and if he has cheated anyone, he will pay them back fourfold. Whereupon, Jesus tells his host, "Today salvation has come to your house."

What is remarkable in this encounter as regards forgiveness is that forgiveness takes the initiative; it precedes repentance. Jesus accepts Zacchaeus prior to his repentance, and in light of this acceptance, Zacchaeus repents of his past actions and vows to repay all those whom he has wronged; his change of heart follows Jesus invitation to share the meal. Thus, there is no "right" time to forgive – we don't wait until someone is ready or until they indicate they are sorry before accepting them.

Two things stand out as Jesus hangs from the cross that particularly relate to forgiveness. One is Jesus' response to the thief who hangs with him, and the other is what Jesus says to those who have nailed him there. The former shows that it is never too late to ask for forgiveness – Jesus never gives up on anyone. And the latter, shows that forgiveness does not set limits; it knows no end.

When Jesus is hung on the cross, two criminals are hung with him, one on either side. One of them mocks Jesus, asking, "If you are the Christ, why don't you save yourself and us," But the other thief rebukes his mockery, asking, "Do you have no fear of God?" And then adds, "You got the same sentence as he did, but in our case we deserved it: we are paying for what we have done, but this man has done nothing wrong." Turning toward

Jesus, he continues, "Jesus, remember me when you come into your kingdom." And Jesus replies, "In truth I tell you, today you will be with me in paradise."

By his response, Jesus indicates that he never gives up on the wrong-doer. While we might be tempted to say to the thief and those who have committed crimes against us or our loved ones, it's too late for you – you've had your chance, Jesus forgives. He does not set limits; his forgiveness has no expiration date.

As Jesus hangs on the cross, jeered and insulted, with a crown of thorns on his head and a puncture wound in his side, it would be understandable if he turns a cold heart toward those who taunt him. With their cruel and insulting actions, he could easily have said they don't deserve my forgiveness - maybe some day they will see the light, maybe when they face their own death, they'll have a sense of sorrow for what they've done, but for now, they're not yet ready for forgiveness. But instead of condemning them, Jesus says, "Father, forgive them for they know not what they do."

Had his focus been only on himself and those who taunted him, there could have been no forgiveness for there was little to see but his own pain and their ignorance and unworthiness. But Jesus' focus is filtered through a very different lens; he sees not only their unworthiness and lack of sorrow for their actions, but also God's unconditional love. He forgives them, not because they deserved it, but because forgiveness is a gift that does not wait for contrition. It is here on the cross that we see forgiveness is the only possibility of escaping the law of the echo – the "tit-for-tat".

It is said we are always echoes – the only question is, "Of what – guilt and retribution or forgiveness and love?" Is our motivation to "get even" or is it to forgive and create a new future? Thankfully, in the end we are not judged solely by our merit, but by a gracious God whose forgiveness Jesus incarnates.

Jesus: The Storyteller

"A story doesn't have to have religious content to make it holy." T. Boomershine

Jesus' parables are intended to show how God is present in everyday life. He uses images like a mustard seed, a woman kneading dough or searching for a lost coin, or a shepherd searching for a lost sheep to remind us that the divine appears in the most ordinary realities.

But while the stories Jesus tells focus on everyday life, they are not just nice, bedtime stories. Many of his stories are quite challenging, and difficult to understand, even for his disciples. Often they subvert prevailing understandings of the chosen and the rejected. The father kills the fatted calf and throws a party, not for the faithful son who stays home and works on the farm, but for the prodigal son who wastes his inheritance. The one who shows compassion and comes to the aid of the man who has been beaten and robbed is not a priest or Levite, both members of the religious community, but a despised Samaritan. The workers in the vineyard who have spent the entire day toiling under the blazing sun are paid the same wage as those who have only worked one hour. Challenging his culture's values, it is not surprising that these parables of Jesus may have contributed to his crucifixion.

Most of us probably tend to think of God as rewarding the good and seeing the bad punished or at least unrewarded. But in the parables of Jesus, rewarding and punishing seem to have much more to do with people's ways of responding. The risk-takers, like those who double their talents, are rewarded, while the one-talent servant who holds on to what the master has given him is sent packing. Jesus admonishes the lawyer seeking eternal life to follow the example of the despised Samaritan, not the priest.

Those rewarded in each of the four sermons that follow are surprising choices. In the parable of the workers in the vineyard, it seems unfair that those who work all day are paid the same as those who only work one hour. Our initial response is to side with the workers who complain about their wage and say "yes" when the owner asks, "*Do you begrudge my generosity*?" Who of us is ready for this radical way of thinking about justice and grace?

For those of us who have a soft-spot for the underdog, it certainly appears in the parable of the talents that the one-talent servant gets the short end of the stick. His punishment would have been understandable had he wasted the talent he was given, but since he saved it and gave it back to his master, his banishment seems unfair, especially when his talent is given to those who already have more. When it comes to using our own talents, how many of us are prepared for this kind of challenge?

Once more, in the parable of the prodigal son, Jesus challenges our idea of who should be rewarded when the party is given for the son who has wasted his inheritance. If this is how the father responds, what is the point of being the good son who stays home? Are any of us ready for this kind of grace, especially if we are the son who stays home?

If we find it amusing to occasionally see the religious community's light dimmed, we may enjoy the parable of the "good" Samaritan. But if the Samaritan were one of our own enemies, would we feel the same way? And as for that beaten man on the side of the road, how many of us would be ready to follow the Samaritan's example, heeding Jesus' words to "Go and do likewise"?

Grumbling About Grace

It was my freshman year at the University of Kansas. My roommate, Phil, and I were both enrolled in an introductory philosophy class. He found the class boring and never seemed to crack a book. I found studying Plato's dialogues fascinating and spent hours mulling over the clever arguments. I asked questions in class; Phil was absent more often than present. I studied hours for the final exam; Phil went to movies. When we received our grades, I could hardly believe the results – I got a "C"; Phil got an "A".

This kind of thing can happen at any time in life, of course. It may happen at school, or on the job, or in some leisure time pursuit. We study longer, work harder, invest twice as much sweat and effort as our neighbor or fellow worker, and the results favor them, not us. What makes this so hard to swallow is that it's contrary to our American way of thinking. We believe people should get what they earn. Though we may not say it out loud, when we work hard, save our money, and take care of our family, we think, if there's a heaven, we've earned it. To our way of thinking, goodness should be rewarded; laziness punished – at least in the next life, if not this one.

The same kind of thinking is in the mind of Peter when he asks Jesus, "What will we get out of being your disciples? We have left everything – work, family, and home, to follow you." Peter wants to know if the cost of following Jesus will be worth the reward.

In reply, Jesus tells this story about an owner of a vineyard who hires laborers at various times during the day. At the close of the day, when those who have worked all day are paid the same wage as those who have only worked one hour, it doesn't seem right. When the employer asks those who complain, "Do you begrudge my generosity?" the answer, in all honesty, is yes. The offense is not at the treatment those who have toiled all day receive. After all, they are paid exactly what they had agreed to work for. Their complaint comes when they observe those who have worked less are paid the same. It's not that they aren't getting what they deserve; it's that the others are getting more. They are offended by grace when its generosity is extended to someone else! How many of us would complain if we were among the group that had labored only one hour?

From the standpoint of economic justice, it is not fair. But Jesus is obviously not talking about economics, but the kingdom of God. Telling this story in response to Peter's asking what will be the disciples' reward for following him, Jesus' answer no doubt challenges them as it does us. If our reward does not correspond to our calculation of what we deserve, why should we expend so much effort? Who wants to be on time, much less start work early, for that kind of employer? Why should we not grumble about this kind of grace? If God sends his rain on the just and the unjust equally, why should we be among the just? If God forgives the Ninevites, why shouldn't we join Jonah in feeling betrayed when he spares them?

Before we answer, at least a couple of things should be noted about this parable: (l) the reward is the same for all workers, and (2) receiving the reward with gratitude seems tied more to what others receive than the number of hours one has worked. To gain a better appreciation of this parable, which upon our first hearing is a very troubling story, let us now take a closer look at each of these.

The idea that the reward is the same for all the workers is a rebuttal of all who would make a special claim on God. It means that seniority and the length of the work day as represented by those who have worked all day do not merit a bonus or any special favor. And the same applies to those who have endured harder working conditions by working in the midday sun – they too, receive no special compensation. And it is true as well for those who might claim a greater need because, in being hired last, they have only been able to work one hour. The reward, regardless of one's claim for either special privilege or special need, remains the same for all. There is no place here for either "work's righteousness" or special treatment for the needy.

In dispensing with the idea of "works righteousness", this parable makes it clear that goodness, as represented by one's labor, is its own reward. If good deeds are only a means to an end, then they can have no intrinsic value. As long as we view heaven as something we earn by our own effort, be it good deeds, prayer, church attendance, or tithing, we shall always be frustrated in our quest for the peace of God. But if our reward is seen as a gift that simply comes with our invitation to work in the vineyard, then we can rejoice and be thankfully employed without questioning the reward someone else may receive.

And if the reward is the same for all, why not arrive early – would it not be preferable to enjoy the company of your master and fellow employees all day instead of just for an hour? Surely, if we were to meet the love of our life, would we not prefer it be early rather than late?

As Jesus tells this story, getting what we feel we deserve is related to the idea we act from. If we think our reward should be governed by how many hours we have worked in relation to our fellow workers, then the number of hours we labor is the critical factor in determining our pay. But if we think our reward will be dependent upon the contract we've signed, then what others may receive is immaterial; what matters is that we are paid the reward called for by our contract.

That the reward is the same for all seems to arise from the grace of the employer, and since grace can never be divided, all receive the same reward. In Jesus' day, there was such a thing as a twelfth of a denari called a pondion; but there is no such thing as a twelfth part of grace. All the workers receive the first prize; there is no second prize. Like being pregnant, you can't be just a little bit pregnant; you either are or you are not.

What is most critical in receiving the reward is saying "yes" to the invitation to work. Those who grumble about the employer's generosity are told to take their pay and go. While they do not lose their wage, they are dismissed from the vineyard, and by implication, from further employment. The problem with making justice the standard for what we receive is that it may cause us to miss the invitation itself. All along they have been in the kingdom; now in their concern for justice, they must depart. When justice becomes our dominant concern in evaluating what we have received, it blinds us to the **value** of what we have received, and may lead us to resent what others get. Thus, when our focus is on our "just desserts", we may lose, not only our temper, but something much more important - the grace we've been given.

This parable offers a radical way of thinking about justice for it challenges our belief that God's chief responsibility is to reward the good and punish the bad. But this story makes clear God's concern is not so much how we stack up with our neighbor, but that we answer the invitation that is offered. When is getting more than our neighbor so important that it keeps us from entering the kingdom of heaven? Perhaps, when we grumble and don't fully appreciate God's grace.

The Sin That Keeps Us Beggars

"In the end, the sin we must all come to grips with is the sin of withholding ourselves. This is the sin that keeps us beggars." These words, found in Elizabeth O'Connor's *The Eighth Day of Creation*, refer to the sad, but unarguable fact that most human beings go through life only partially aware of the full range of their abilities.

For various reasons, like the one-talent fellow in Jesus' parable about the talents, we hold on to our gifts and talents rather than putting them to use. It may be self-doubt because we're not sure our talents are adequate, or at least, not as good as someone else's. Like Moses, when God calls him to deliver his people from their Egyptian slavery, we make excuses, suggesting we are slow of speech or others are more qualified. We think our talents are too small in comparison to another's, or we resist using what we've been given because we're upset that our gifts seem so insignificant; others have more.

Or maybe we hold on to our gifts because we fear criticism. No one wants to appear stupid or foolish. Yet, how many times do we remain ignorant because we are not willing to come forward and say we do not understand something. We are like the students who, when the teacher asks if everyone understands, remain silent even though there is much we don't understand. How many times do we unnecessarily hurt ourselves because we do not want to admit our inner feelings. Something that recently happened to a friend of mine who hurt his back lifting something too heavy because he was afraid to say he needed help, and feared his girl friend might think he was a weakling if he did.

Sometimes it is this fear of rejection that keeps our gifts bottled up. In a *New York Times Book Review*, Edward Dahlberg wrote poignantly of lost opportunities for relationship when he reflected on his encounters with the writer, Theodore Dreiser. He had longed to know Dreiser, but when he thought of getting in touch with the man, he pictured him engaged in writing another masterpiece and felt he could not interrupt him. Finally, Dahlberg took the risk and asked Dreiser to come to his apartment for coffee. Listen now, as I share Dalhberg's piercing lines in the story of their relationship. "My meetings with Dreiser continued, but I was always of the mind that I was ravaging his precious time. Long after his death, I read in a biographical study of Dreiser that at the time we became acquainted, his closest friend had died and he hoped that Edward Dahlberg might take his place. What a shock it was to read that one devastating line!"

Are there times in each of our lives when we too have short-circuited a potential friendship because we feared we might be imposing on someone's time; times when we hesitate to call and ask someone to share a walk or a cup of coffee because we know how busy they are? How many times do we lose opportunities for knowledge and friendship that too often result in misunderstanding and loneliness?

Whatever our reason for withholding our self and our gifts, be it fear of rejection or criticism or self-doubt, it is often encased in fear. Perhaps, like the one-talent man in this morning's story, we fear what will be demanded of us, and decide that protecting what we have is more important than risking its loss. We resist the recognition of our assets because, once recognized, they must be used. It is much easier to be committed to God in the abstract than at the point of a particular gift; easier to say I support the church with my gifts than I will teach Sunday school; easier to say I support a friend for political office than to say I will ring doorbells.

But regardless of the reasons for our reluctance to use our gifts, our gifts make claims upon us and must be used; otherwise they go to waste. In this sense, we human beings are akin to the battery in a flashlight; unused, it corrodes. Like someone has said, "Badness is goodness damned up." And as this parable of Jesus makes clear, the only talents that God cannot use are those we bury. When we refuse to use our gifts, our potential is unrealized because the gifts and talents we have only reach their fullest potential when they are exercised. And even more important, like this one-talent man, when we bury our gifts, we may never enter into the joy of the master.

If you, like me, have a soft-spot for underdogs, you probably feel the one-talent servant got the short-end of the stick. Not only does he have less to start with, but even what he has is taken from him. It doesn't seem fair that the rich get richer, and the poor lose even what they have. What, after all, has this poor fellow done that's so bad? Has he not given the master back what the master gave him? He didn't lose it or make it less valuable. Isn't the master just being mean and arbitrary?

But before we condemn the master it may be important to ask if the one-talent servant's image of the master is accurate. Is the master the hard-hearted man of the third servant's description? Does he reap where he does not sow, or is he gracious and generous as he was to the first two servants? Which view is correct?

The key point seems to be what the master does with the money he takes back. He doesn't keep it for himself, but rather gives it away to encourage those who have used well what they have been given the first time. It isn't his own gain that concerns him, but rather the way the servants each treat what they have received.

What this suggests is that being cautious and safe is not always to be commended. The parable seems to be directed at those who try to make sure of their own rightness before God by understanding goodness as not sinning - not taking any chances of offending God. The one-talent servant's downfall begins with his fear of the master; fearing what may be demanded of him, he buries his talent. Protecting what he had was more important than risking its loss, but by holding onto it and not risking, he lost even what he had. Knowing the master reaped where he did not sow, he should have realized merely giving him back what he had been given would not be satisfactory.

What counts most in life, according to this parable, is not the number of talents we possess, but how we use them. The one-talent man is not condemned for having just one talent, but for not using it. While the distribution of talents is never equal, we are all called to some responsibility. In God's scheme of things, we all have some part to play. The key is not the number of talents we possess, but what we do with what we have. The only gifts we need ever grieve are those we bury for they are the only ones God cannot use, and they are the ones that keep us beggars.

The richness of a gift should never be discounted because it is common. Mary Schram in her book, *Gifts and Graces*, tells about the importance the gift of a simple hug can have. A man who had recently lost his spouse was doing his laundry in the basement of a large apartment complex. Another apartment dweller, knowing the man's loss, went over and gave him a hug of understanding. And as the widower told his son later that day in a conversation over the phone, "That hug meant the world to me." There are no unholy gifts; each needs to be used for the harmony of God's symphony to be heard in all its richness. Whatever the instrument we may play, when it is not played, the music the world hears is never as good as the composer intended.

Exile and Homecoming

It's a theme dealt with in countless books, but perhaps no where more strikingly than in this story of the prodigal son. Some have called this parable the greatest of all Jesus' teachings as it so beautifully encompasses the themes of exile and homecoming.

The story revolves around a father and his two sons - the younger, who takes his inheritance and leaves home, and the older, who stays home to work on his father's farm. The story's climax occurs upon the younger son's return home when we see the very different attitudes the father and his two sons each bring to it - sorrow, joy, and jealous displeasure are all on vivid display.

In the beginning, as we follow the younger son on his journey, we see the freedom and independence he enjoys; but then, gradually it eludes his grasp. As first, he lives in a grand style, with plenty of money and friends. But for some reason, all this seems to dwindle into nothing. No reason is given, but perhaps his "good" life was dependent upon the things he could buy and when his resources dwindled, so did his friendships. At any rate, he soon finds himself broke and alone, and finally has to hire himself out to a pig farmer.

One thing about his situation that he seems to overlook is that everything he owns has been a gift from his father. His possessions, money, clothes, shoes, food, and drink – all have come from his father's inheritance. In themselves they are good things, but as he uses them they become his undoing, for the story says, "he squandered them in loose living." And so when a famine comes upon the land, he hires himself out to a pig farmer just to survive..

At this point, it dawns on him that the servants on his father's farm are better off than he is, and he ponders the thought, "How many of my father's hired men have all the food they want and more, while I am dying of hunger." So he decides he will return home, admit the error of his ways to his father, and ask to be hired back as one of his father's servants.

In commenting upon his decision to return home, Helmut Thielicke, the great German theologian, suggests that the son's choice is not merely motivated by disgust with his current situation, but also by homesickness. Hence, the son is not just turning away from something, but he is turning back home. Disgust with himself could have made a cynic of the son, but it is unlikely cynicism alone could have shown him the way back home. His return home was not just because the far country made him sick;

he turned back home, realizing he could have a better life there than what he was finding in the "far country."

Every age has its own "far country," and so has ours. All the estrangement the younger son feels - his diversions, hunger, and empty feelings, are all a part of this "far country" experience. We may, of course, use the abundant resources of this bountiful earth that are our inheritance without taking into account the Creator who has given them, and we may still believe in a "good" God. But like the younger son, we too may be left with an empty feeling and a longing for home when the diversions we at first enjoy, be they country club, boat, and exotic vacations or something far less grand, eventually lose their luster and become less satisfying.

So now the younger son heads for home. But how will the father receive him? What will he say? And what will he himself say when suddenly he is before his father? Will he say, "Father, I grew more mature in the far country. I have learned to be responsible and now I have grown up and become a man. I now realize how wonderful home is, and would like to return." Jesus' parable says nothing about this. The son who comes home says only, "Father, I have sinned against heaven and before you; I no longer deserve to be called your son; treat me as one of your hired men." In essence, he says he has no claim on his father whatsoever.

The fact that the younger son is taken back has nothing to do with his maturity, but solely to do with the graciousness of his father's love. He has no claim on his father's love. That he is received with open arms and rejoicing is a gift. After all, there was no guarantee that the father would so readily and totally forgive him.

A story is told of a certain prodigal son who, on turning up in the far country of another parish, was advised by the minister there to go home and let his father "kill the fatted calf" for him. The prodigal obeyed, and months later, meeting the same minister again, was asked if the father had indeed killed the fatted calf for him. "No," came the reply, "but he almost killed the prodigal son."

It is this latter attitude that characterizes the feeling of the older son when he is told of his younger brother's return. Instead of sharing in his father's happiness, the older son refuses to even come to the house to see his brother. Anger and self-pity come over him as he complains to the father, "You know how I have slaved for you all these years; *I* have never disobeyed your orders, yet you never so much as gave me a kid for a feast with my friends. But now this son of yours turns up, after running through your money with his loose women, and you kill the fatted calf for him." The fact that the elder son feels cheated reveals that he sees his relationship with his father more as a kind of obedience than a source of joy. Like some people whose religion has made them dutiful, his service to his father has robbed him of a sense of joy. For him, his father's love has been so constant that it has been taken for granted.

Often we judge this elder son harshly for his bitterness. We see him as a jealous mama's boy who stayed home rather than risk the adventure of his younger brother. But we should be careful how harshly we judge him - first, because we may find more of ourselves in his jealousy than we like to admit, and second, because the father's response shows us something different. The father does not admonish his son and criticize him for his poor attitude; instead he reminds him that "all I have is yours," and adds, "it was only right that we should celebrate and rejoice, for your brother was dead and has come to life; he was lost and is found."

While this elder son passes judgment on his younger brother, do we in turn pass judgment on him? If our generosity is only expressed for the deserving, how generous are we? It is one thing to be appreciative of excellence; it is quite another to be sympathetic to those who fail. The elder son's shortcomings like his prodigal brother's simply serve as a backdrop for the infinite goodness of the father. While we may be prone to see the younger son's return as cheap capitulation and the elder son's faithfulness as nothing more than dull respectability, the father sees things quite differently; for him, his younger son's return is a joyous homecoming and the older son's staying home is faithful dependability. The father's love spans the whole scale of human possibilities. Whichever son (or daughter) we may be, we can rest assured we have not been excluded from the father's love – for his love has no boundaries, and in his heart there is a place for all. Wherever we may be in exile, he stands ready to rejoice in all our homecomings – whether we come from the "far country" or have been the one who dutifully stayed home.

Who Is the Neighbor?

In Dostoyevskky's great novel, *The Brothers Karamazov*, Father Zossima, a saint in the best sense of the word, is visited by a woman who has, she says, great dreams of serving humanity in general but who fails miserably when it comes to loving particular human beings. After listening to her, Zossima tells her, "Love in action is a harsh and dreadful thing compared with love in dreams; love in dreams is performed rapidly and in the sight of all, but love in reality is slow and laborious and not always recognized."

It is this kind of on-going, silent caring that Christ tells about in this story of the good Samaritan. Love, as Jesus portrays it in the story, has nothing to do with what we may think of another person, whether they are attractive or deserving, or whether we respect them; love is rather a silent, on-going care for another person's well-being.

This story of the good Samaritan arises in response to a lawyer's question. The lawyer is wanting to know what love means – not just according to scripture, but in real life. He knows how scripture answers his question – "to inherit eternal life, one must love, first God, and then one's neighbor." But when it comes to the neighbor, what he wants to know is where to draw the line? So he asks Jesus, "Who is my neighbor?"

We should not too quickly dismiss his question as being too simplistic; it is after all quite reasonable. Think of the daily demands that other people make on our limited resources of time, energy, and money. Who among those asking for our help can we exclude from neighborly care and still maintain a clear conscience?

Every day, for instance, we meet people who want a little bit of our attention and sometimes our money. Some days, just being there for family, church members, friends, and strangers on the street who ask for help seems overwhelming. And beyond them, what about all the others - the almost daily requests from various charities and social service agencies; the hundreds of hungry and hurting we see each night on television or read about in the newspaper. There is only so much of us to go around; we can not help all of them – hardly even a few of them. Yet, one does not want to go around all day feeling guilty. Lines do need to be drawn. So, as the lawyer asks, who can we set outside the limits of our neighborly concern without forfeiting the claim to be an ethical person?

For an answer, Jesus tells this story. A certain man was going down from Jerusalem to Jericho when robbers attacked him, beat him, stripped him of his clothes, and left him half dead. He lays there naked, barely conscious, in pain, and needing help. Stripped of his clothes, which might help identify his social class and village, those passing by are unable to tell much about him – only that he lies bleeding beside the road.

A priest and a Levite, an individual who would have had hereditary privileges and duties in the temple, pass by – the kind of people most likely to respond since it is the business of the religious to help the wounded. But they are human, and like all of us, may have had other priorities. Maybe they are hurrying to their temple duties, which they regard as ultimately more significant than helping a single injured person. The injured, the poor, and the sick will always be in the world, but the praise of the Creator and Sustainer of all things living must never cease. Or, they may think the man is already dead and are concerned that by touching him they will make themselves legally unclean and so unfit for their responsibilities. And it is not inconceivable that they know of someone even more desperately ill – perhaps a friend or a relative – whom they feel has a greater claim on their help.

And yet again, what if it is a ruse? Out here on a lonely road – maybe this is how the robbers trick people into stopping. And then, when one draws near to see how he can help, the man on the ground grabs you, and others jump out from behind a little mound and hit you on the back of the head. Then you will be the man in the ditch! Better to find some other neighbor to help, and try to forget this one.

So let's not be too critical of the priest and the Levite, for like them, we have our own good reasons for passing by on the other side. Surely the wounded man is either stupid or ill-informed; everyone knows this is a dangerous road, and not one to be traveled alone. If he is in trouble, it's his own fault. Is not this how we dismiss helping those on welfare? They deserve their fate since they are lazy and unwilling to work; or they prefer to live off welfare and don't know how to budget; or they buy expensive clothes and gamble their money away - either at the casino or playing bingo.

And again, like the priest and Levite, we also are pressed for time and don't want to get hurt. What if the injured has AID's? If we touch him, might we not get infected from his blood? And if we come to his aid, might we not get hauled into court as a witness to a crime, and have to take time off work – time that will most likely be docked from our paycheck? So why not just write out a check to the United Good Neighbor fund and let those properly trained come to the aid of those in need? After all, as busy as I am, it is easier to write out a check than stop and try to help.

Clearly, our reasons for passing by are numerous; but whatever they may be, Jesus reminds us there is one who stops. He is a Samaritan, who in that time was an enemy to those to whom Jesus tells the story. Shockingly, it is this historic, mixed-race enemy who exemplifies Jesus' teaching that we are to emulate God's love by loving our enemies. This man who is of a different religion, the one we would least expect to stop, is the one who cleans the beaten man's wounds, bandages him, carries him to an inn, and says he'll pay the bill and be back in a couple of days if there is more to be paid.

So how well does this story of Jesus meet the lawyer's concern? The lawyer, we remember, has really been asking, "Who is not my neighbor?" His concern is whom can I not treat with neighborly love and still manage to be a law-fulfilling, respectable person? Where can I draw the line? Jesus, in this story of the good Samaritan, shifts the lawyer's question from, "Who is, or is not, my neighbor?" to "Who is the neighbor?" Thus, the neighbor is no longer an object – someone I must love; the neighbor is the subject – someone who does mercy. As the good Samaritan illustrates, the true neighbor acts with compassion for whomever needs his or her help. Are they deserving? Is there risk involved? Do I have the time? It does not matter; those who would be a part of God's kingdom are called to act in love - a love which refuses to walk by on the other side and is not put off by the unattractiveness of the situation.

Do we dare, or even want to be, this free? No doubt, there have been times when we have known moments where we felt this power and freedom, and ventured beyond those boundaries of self-concern – those boundaries that limit and keep us from moving toward that frontier where Jesus proclaims the kingdom of God is truly breaking in. These are important moments for they are the times when we have stopped trying to be merely ethical, like the lawyer, and have allowed a positive love rather than our worries and busyness, or a defensive concern with morality, to be our guide. Let us pray that with God's help we may all keep moving toward that frontier that has no boundaries.

Jesus: the Healer

"Health is the greatest of all our possessions." B. Bickerstaff

Many stories in the New Testament revolve around the power of Jesus to heal. These accounts of healing include people with a variety of maladies, including the deaf and dumb, the blind, the lame, the mentally ill, and the diseased. Some people attribute Jesus' healing power to his divinity, some see it as a result of prayer and faith, others view the healings in more psychological terms, and still others as creations of the gospel writers themselves for the purpose of demonstrating Jesus' exalted status as the Son of God, the messianic figure who will bring in the reign of God.

Whatever explanation we may use, it is important to examine each story in the gospel setting in which we find it. Some healing stories are surrounded by disputes about Jesus' authority; does his power to heal come from God or the devil? In other stories, conflict with the religious leaders over the law is central. For the Pharisees, Jesus' healing on the Sabbath violates the Sabbath law and therefore is wrong. In nearly all the people whom Jesus heals, the person healed plays a significant role. For the man lying by the pool in Bethesda, it is a matter of surrendering his illusion someone else will come to his aid, and taking responsibility himself for his healing. With the man blind since birth, it is an unquestioning obedience; he washes himself in the Pool of Siloam, unhesitatingly acting on what Jesus tells him to do. And in the case of Bartimaeus, it is a cry for mercy, refusing to be silenced by the crowd of on-lookers, and telling Jesus what he wants.

The role of Jesus in the New Testament healing stories varies with the situation encountered. In the story of the man crippled for thirty-eight year, Jesus does not play a very sympathetic role; he expresses neither sorrow nor sympathy for the man's condition, but rather challenges him to take responsibility for where he is – first, by asking him if he wants to recover, and then, telling him to rise to his feet, pick up his mat, and walk. In essence, Jesus challenges the man's self understanding, suggesting that waiting for someone to place him in the healing waters is the very reason for his failure to get well; he is a victim of his own false dependence upon another.

In the story of the man blind from birth, Jesus plays a more direct role in restoring his sight, emphasizing to his disciples the importance of prayer. The reason for the man's blindness, Jesus tells them, is the fault neither of his parents nor the man himself, but is rather so the works of God might be revealed in healing him. With this as an introduction, Jesus spits on the ground, makes a paste with the spittle, puts it on the blind man's eyes, and tells him to go and wash in the Pool of Siloam. Here Jesus acts directly, assuming the man will do as told. Any prior questions or get-acquainted conversation is simply omitted in the gospel writer's telling of the story. If the role of Jesus in healing the cripple at Bethesda is to challenge, here it is to command.

With Bartimaeus, Jesus plays a much more sympathetic role. First, he recognizes the blind man's voice and calls him forward; secondly, he asks him what he wants. Unlike the other two healing stories, Jesus does not direct the action, but allows the one wanting help to take the lead. Bartimaeus is not told to do anything in order to be healed; Jesus simply recognizes his cry for mercy, and his refusal to be silenced, and tells him, "Your faith has saved you," affirming the man's initiative in effecting his own healing.

Beyond Illusion to Faith

What is involved in living a meaningful life? Throughout history, theologians and philosophers have offered various ideas. Some have focused on performing certain actions, such as service to others or work that is challenging and productive. Others have looked at relationships as the key, suggesting a meaningful life is best found in a loving relationship. And still others have insisted the answer lies not in our **doing**, but in our **being.** Here the answer is to be found within ourselves, and is more a matter of self-acceptance and appreciating what we already are, not what we acquire.

Whatever answer we might find meaningful for ourselves, surely two key ingredients we might include would be friends and good health, each of which is found in the New Testament story we've just heard. The key question this story raises is does the health of this man who has been crippled for thirty-eight years depend upon a friend helping him into the healing waters, or is this a false dependency and an illusion that prevents the man from taking responsibility for his life, and thus recovering his health.

As the story goes, there's a man in the crowd who has an illness which has lasted thirty-eight years. Jesus comes upon the crowd and focuses his attention on this man, seemingly aware his condition has existed for a long time. Abruptly, Jesus asks the man, "Do you want to be well again?" The question seems somewhat of an affront, as it implies the man may not really be serious about wanting to be healed. And in this sense, it even appears to question the man's integrity.

But more than the man's integrity is at stake; indeed, the very basis of his self-understanding is being challenged. The last thirty-eight years of his life have been lived with the belief that his health and well-being are dependent upon someone else – someone who can place him in the water at the appropriate moment. Hence, he has refused to accept his life as given, preferring to pin his hopes for a meaningful life on some one else and a future event. And as a result, he has become enslaved by his past illness, whatever it is.

Before continuing with this story, it might be useful to ask if there are not places where we can identify with this man who has been crippled by his illness for thirty-eight years. Are there not instances where we, like this man, have pointed to someone else to give our life its meaning? Places where we have looked to some person or some future event like a magic pool of water - the Prince Charming who will rescue us from whatever is lacking in our current life and bring us happiness; the silver bullet that will solve whatever ails us. In our society, it may be a certain education reform, change of government, or scientific discovery. In the church, it might be the greater involvement of young people, a new minister, or a million dollar endowment – all things which might be nice, but also may be an excuse that locks us into the status quo, and in doing so, become the very thing keeping us from changing our present condition.

If there are places in our life where we have been dependent upon someone or something else to give our life meaning, if there are times when we have refused to accept our life as it is given, perhaps we too need to be challenged by Jesus' question, "Do you want to be well again?" While we may all look to the future for a better life, we may first need to accept and take responsibility for the present, whatever problems it may contain.

The answer the crippled man in John's gospel gives to Jesus' challenge is more a lament than an affirmative response, "I have no one to put me in the pool…someone else always gets in the pool before me." Here then, is a man who seemingly wants to be cured, but finds himself mercilessly alone. But if sympathy is what he wants, it is not what he gets. Seeming to disregard his lament, Jesus tells the man, "Rise to your feet, pick up your mat, and walk." This is a far cry from a sympathetic answer, yet it is in this response that we can begin to discern where healing may be found, and what it may mean, not only for this man, but for ourselves – to see and understand who we are in terms of the <u>gift</u> <u>and</u> <u>demand</u> of God's love.

The **gift** is the **unconditional acceptance** of the man **as he is**. So what if he's been incapacitated by his illness for thirty-eight years – it doesn't matter! So he has been completely dependent upon someone else and has meekly accepted his life can't be changed without another's help – it doesn't matter! In communicating God's love, Jesus is saying, "Your life is okay the way it is. You don't need to wait for someone else to put you in the pool to make your life good." In other words, God accepts this man and us as we are; our limitations are not a reason to sit life out. God's gift of acceptance is freely given. But if the gift is to be accepted, there must be an appropriate response for it to become meaningful. Jesus says we must quit waiting for someone else to make us whole; all that is needed is to simply "pick up our mats (excuses), and walk."

A friend of mine tells the story that his aunt once won a new car at a raffle, but having never learned to drive, she couldn't use it without acquiring her driver's license. The demand that comes with the gift of God's love is not that we learn to drive, of course, but it does demand that we die to our illusions. If we are to pick up our life and live it, we must stop waiting for someone else to give our life its sense of worth. If we are interested in improving the quality of air we breathe, we may need to begin more carefully choosing our transportation in accord with its impact on the environment. If we are really interested in seeing the church come alive, we must stop waiting for the "young people", or a new minister, or some wealthy donor's endowment; the church's renewal is in our hands, not someone else's.

This **demand** to **die to our illusions** is never an easy thing to accept. Most of the time when the going gets tough we would much rather live in the past or dream about a different future rather than take responsibility for the present. But the gift and demand of God's love tell us our life is not in the future, but the present; it is not to be found in some other circumstance, but in those at hand. And indeed, our life is not even to be sought after, for it is already given.

Our preference for a different financial status or our complaining that we are "too old" or "too young" simply do not stand up when Jesus says, "Rise to your feet, pick up your mat, and walk." Our preference for another day, another spouse, or another church is all too often simply a refusal to accept our present life as it is given. To live in Christ means to celebrate the reign of God's love in the present – not to await some meaning to be revealed in the future. It is in giving ourselves wholly to God's love and surrendering our illlusions that we realize our true well-being and discover life's deepest meaning.

In the fifties, the church may have been packed every Sunday, but it's not so today. If we are to accept our present life, then we must die to the illusion that strength lies in numbers, and realize that whatever strength we have lies in our individual commitments today. Let us accept the gift and demand of God's unconditional love.

A Question of Belief

It is the longest and most involved story of healing in the Bible, encompassing as it does the entire ninth chapter of John's gospel. It tells about Jesus restoring the sight of a man who has been blind from birth, and in the process raises several important questions: Why is the man blind? What is involved in the recovery of his sight? And, how do his parents and the Pharisees respond to his healing?

Back in 1968 as a graduate student at Indiana University, I lived in the Wesley Foundation apartment and became close friends with the campus minister, whose office was next door. Gil was a respected and well-loved campus minister, who in the midst of numerous student demonstrations and campus unrest, was well known as a courageous, reconciling voice of reason and justice. One summer night I helped Gil and his young family as they packed their VW bus and headed to Maine for a vacation. Three nights later, I received a phone call that shook the foundations of my faith - Gil had died in a drowning accident. The news hit me like a bolt of lightening – why had this happened? What kind of God allows such a thing to happen?

Jesus' disciples raise a similar question in this morning's text, "Rabbi, why was this man born blind? Who sinned - this man or his parents, that he should have been born blind?" In their eyes, blindness (tragedy) is a result of someone's sin. Reflecting the prevailing attitude at the time, the disciples view blindness as a punishment, either caused by the sin of the parents or the man himself. But Jesus refuses to look for a culprit; in his eyes, suffering is not a deserved punishment, but a place where the works of God might be made manifest. His focus is not on placing blame, but seeing how God is present in the midst of suffering.

While the healing of the blind man is not without its cost, it basically involves an unquestioning, active obedience. When Jesus tells him to go and wash in a certain pool, he doesn't ask, "Why?" He neither questions Jesus' authority nor the healing powers of the pool's water; he goes and does as Jesus instructs him. Without knowing the outcome, his response is an immediate, active obedience – a response that is in direct contrast to that of the Pharisees, who question Jesus' authority, and his parents, who defer their response to someone else. And as a result of his unhesitating response, he now can see.

But instead of celebrating the blind man's recovery of sight, the Pharisees, who as religious leaders should be most appreciative of this man's recovery of sight, prefer to look at the fact that the healing takes place on the Sabbath, and is thus a violation of their religious law. Sidetracked by legality, they are so concerned about keeping the law that they lose sight of human need. For them, Christ is no man of God because he breaks the Sabbath law. A healthy skepticism about life may be helpful if it serves to bring us closer to the truth, but this kind of skepticism which the Pharisees exhibit is more an effort to discredit someone. Thus, it is not surprising when the blind man asks if they want to become Jesus' disciples, they become defensive, and rather than listen to the blind man's account of his healing, they expel him from the synagogue. They, like many of us, find it easier to deal with a problem if you don't have to face it.

None of us would like to identify ourselves with the Pharisees, and yet there are times when we too allow ourselves to get "hung up" on legalities. Are there not times when we can get so involved in arguing over church doctrine and theological interpretation that we fail to take seriously Christ's call to obey his teachings. If we really want to participate in the church as an agent of reconciliation and healing, we will not be put off by someone who has a different understanding of the virgin birth than our own.

When the parents are asked to acknowledge that the blind man is their son, they have no trouble saying, "yes", but when they are asked how his sight has been restored, they defer the question, saying, "Ask him, he is old enough he can speak for himself." Not wishing to mention Jesus' role in the healing since the Jews have made it clear that anyone who acknowledges Jesus as the Christ will be banned from the synagogue, they choose to defer the question about the recovery of their son's sight.

The response of the parents, deferring the question, is one often heard today, especially in a time of the specialist and technical expert. Like the parents, we can defer the question, claiming we are not as qualified or knowledgeable as someone else. But just because we are not qualified in a technical sense does not mean we need to abdicate our moral responsibilities. The pastor may have spent more time studying theology, but that does not mean he is automatically the best equipped member of the congregation when it comes to ministering to someone's needs. The person who designed the artificial heart is certainly more qualified than we to see that it works, but that does not mean we should leave the decision about when a heart transplant should be performed entirely up to doctors. The conducting of war is one that the military expert is far better prepared to deal with than most of us, but when a war should be waged is the responsibility of everyone who values peace. In a world where technically it is possible to do almost anything, it becomes more important than ever that we, the nonexperts, do not abdicate our role in helping set priorities and determining how technology will be used.

One interesting aspect of this story is to see how the blind man's understanding of Jesus changes as he is questioned by the Pharisees. When first asked who has healed him, his response is simply, "The man called Jesus." But the more he is questioned, the more he comes to realize Jesus is perhaps someone more than just another man. Thinking that Jesus is someone who must have a special relationship to God, he initially calls him a prophet; but later, after Jesus asks him if he believes in the Son of Man and explains this is who he is, he calls him, "Lord," and worships him. In the end, he sees Jesus as the Son of Man, the one whom the Jews believe will bring the ultimate triumph of God's reign.

In looking at the blind man's recovery of sight, it is worth noting that Jesus becomes his Lord, first through active obedience, and then in standing up to critical questioning from those who doubt Jesus' role in his recovery. Often we think that putting our faith in God will make life easier, but as this story illustrates, this is not necessarily the case. The blind man's discipleship is not cheap; it comes at great cost since it means the loss of some friends, the embarrassment of his parents, the rejection from the temple, and loss of income - since he could no longer beg for a living, he must now find a job.

Following Jesus does not mean we are automatically rewarded with happiness and popularity. For the blind man, trust in Jesus brings, not only healing, but pain and loss. So when we are asked about our relationship to Jesus, we need to consider our response carefully. Like the Pharisees, we can argue about his authority; like the parents, we can defer the question; or like the blind man, we can simply go where he calls us. Our answer will determine whether we merely admire him as a great man, dismiss him entirely, or serve him as Lord. Perhaps, the most important question this story raises for each of us today is not whether Jesus opened the eyes of the blind man, but whether he can open our eyes.

A Faith That Heals

A crowd gathers alongside the dusty road. Rumor has it the miracle-worker, Jesus, will soon pass by. Lost in the crowd is a blind beggar named Bartimaeus. There is nothing to suggest his life is about to change, or this is a day he will always remember.

Can we imagine what life must have been like for Bartimaeus. The community has long since forgotten how he lost his sight. Whether it was an accident or some disease, no one seems to know. But Bartimaeus remembers it like it was yesterday. How can he ever forget the change it has brought?

The adjustment has been difficult. In the beginning, there was anger and more than a few questions. *"How could this happen? Why me? What have I done to deserve this? What kind of future do I have?"* Anger, recrimination, self-pity – they were all abundantly present. But feeling sorry for yourself doesn't change anything; getting angry and blaming take a lot of energy. And so, in time Bartimaeus decides to make the most of it – to tough it out. His life will be forever changed, but it has not ended.

He discovers most people are sympathetic to his plight so long as he doesn't say or do anything to upset them. But being blind greatly reduces one's job possibilities. In that day, unless your family is wealthy, begging is the primary means of support. It may sound easy, but it isn't. Even when we need it, asking for help is difficult for most of us. As time goes by, Bartimaeus learns to cope. In fact, he learns to beg quite nicely; he knows when to speak, when to keep quiet, and how to be properly grateful.

But accepting one's limitations and adjusting one's lifestyle doesn't always bring satisfaction. Indeed, the more successful he becomes, the more lonely and isolated he feels. As long as he is a "proper" beggar, people give him what he needs to live. But he wants something more than just to make a living. He wants to see things – the birds that sing, the dogs that bark, the stars at night, the changing colors of the leaves, the eyes and expressions on the faces of people. He wants to be something more than a beggar the rest of his life. He is tired of sitting by the side of the road with his hand outstretched, saying, "Thank you."

The day Jesus comes by it all comes to a head. Bartimaeus is tired of pretending everything is okay. He is tired of begging; always saying and doing what other people expect. He is simply fed up with being isolated and lonely. He has heard that Jesus is a healer – that, in fact, he has enabled the lame to walk, the deaf to hear, and the blind to see. And so, when Jesus comes by, he lets go of all his fears and pent-up frustrations – his fear of what it might look like to cry out for help; his fear of what others might think. And so, with all his might, he begins to shout, "Jesus, Son of David, have mercy on me." When the crowd tries to silence him, telling him to be quiet, he only shouts all the louder, "Jesus, Son of David, have mercy on me."

Like those in the crowd who surround Bartimaeus, there is in all of us something that wants to silence anything that will make us uncomfortable; a voice that says, "It is better to be nice than honest," or "If you don't have anything good to say, don't say it." But the story of Bartimaes reminds us Jesus listens, not to those who call for silence, but to the one who cries out in pain.

"Call him." The crowd grows quiet, then someone says, "Bartimaeus, he is calling you." Throwing off his cloak, Bartimaeus jumps up, and with the people in front moving out of his way, approaches where Jesus is standing. "What do you want me to do for you?" Jesus asks. "Master, I want my sight back," comes the simple reply. "Go," says Jesus, "your faith has saved you."

This story of Bartimaeus sounds so simple, but is it true? There is no laying on of hands; no repentance or confession of faith. When Jesus tells Bartimaeus his faith has saved him, what faith is he talking about? Bartimaeus has made no confession of faith; he simply asks to have his sight back. How can this be called a faith that heals?

It may not be what comes to mind when we think of faith, but the faith that heals Bartimaeus has a clear recognition of need, a willingness to ask for help, and a trust that Jesus can provide it. While these may not be the ingredients we generally associate with faith, this story suggests they merit a closer look.

Clearly, a key component of Bartimaeus' healing involves his crying out his pain to Jesus. Had he remained silent, no healing could have happened. Until his timidity in asking for help is overcome, his life will simply continue as a blind beggar. All of which suggests that our own hesitation in asking for help needs to be confronted. Unless we move beyond our fear of what others may think, and our pretension everything is alright when it's not, we may never find the healing that can make us whole.

For many of us, overcoming this fear and pretension is difficult. We fear others will think we are weak if we ask for help, and we seem to prefer living with the illusion that silent suffering is noble. But if we are to move toward the kind of faith that can make us whole, like Bartimaeus, we need to confront our timidity and fear and give up this illusion that "gutting it out" is noble.

And we also need to guard against silencing others who may embarrass us with their cries for help; to stop asking if they are "deserving", and fretting because they are disturbing our peace. It's a fine line between who is and who isn't deserving? But who's to say? Jesus never raises the question with those who hurt. The good Samaritan Jesus talks about never questions whether the beaten man deserves help. Jesus never asks the demon-possessed how they got that way; what drove them up the wall. When Bartimaeus cries out for mercy, Jesus doesn't question his need; he simply asks him what he wants.

Bartimaeus answers without beating around the bush; he simply says, "I want my sight back." This clear recognition of need is often a problem for many of us. We lack clarity about what we want or we want something outside ourselves to make us whole. But as this Bartimaeus story suggests, our need is more likely something on the inside (like sight) than something outside (like money). Jesus simply evokes the inner resources of Bartimaeus to heal himself; he does nothing to make Bartimaeus dependent upon him. He takes no credit for himself, but simply sends him on his way with an affirmation, "Your faith has saved you."

Like Bartimaeus, we yearn for a faith to set us free and make us whole. It is one of the main reasons we gather here on Sunday, and one of the central promises of the Christian faith. But we hold back – too timid to ask for help, fearing what others think. And so we pretend everything is alright, even when it's not. But then one day, Jesus' voice, spoken by a spouse or fellow worker, or perhaps even a stranger, asks us what we want. We want a lot of things, of course, but maybe none more than to have a faith like Bartimaeus – a faith that lets go all our fears because it's willing to trust completely in what Jesus embodies – the love that accepts and affirms us where we are and has the power to call forth that voice in ourselves that can truly heal and make us whole.

Jesus: The Miracle-Worker

"Miracles are not the cause of faith; they are the result of faith." H. Fosdick

The Bible is filled with miracles; from the parting of the Red Sea to Christ walking on water and feeding the multitudes with two fish and five loaves, miracle stories abound. But while miracles were an aid to the faith of the ancient Hebrews and early Christians, to our science-oriented, modern age they are often stumbling blocks to our faith, looked upon with suspicion and embarrassment.

Our modern mind-set has trouble with a God who can change the order of the universe upon a whim. In that kind of world nobody can count on anything. It would be nice if anytime we were in trouble, God could work another miracle, but this is not the way God works. To be sure there are some church-goers who resist the modern way of thinking, or at least modify it to read: miracles do not happen now, but in Bible times they did. And there are also Christian fundamentalists who claim that if a person doesn't believe in them, his or her faith is suspect.

But most theologians do not believe the purpose of the miracles is to test our faith. From their standpoint, the importance of the miracles is to establish God's authority. In John's gospel, when Jesus is asked why the man was born blind, he responds by saying it is so God's power might be revealed in healing him. Miracles, from this perspective, are to be regarded as signs of God's saving activity – crossing the Red Sea is God's deliverance of the Israelites from their Egyptian bondage, feeding the five thousand is not so much about relieving someone's physical hunger as a sign of God's power to satisfy our deepest needs, and the exorcism of demons is less the expulsion of some sinister force than a sign of God's triumph over the forces of evil.

For Jesus, miracles were of modest importance. To the blind man whose sight he restored, Christ said, "See that no one hears about this." To the Pharisees who demanded he show them a sign from heaven of his miraculous power, he said, "No sign shall be given." And on the cross, when some in the crowd mocked him, saying, "He saved others, let him save himself if he is the Christ of God," he is unwilling to make a demonstration of any miraculous power. For Jesus, his own personal safety and deliverance do not merit a miracle.

Jesus is not so much interested in having people believe in miracles, but as the sermons that follow make clear, he is interested in seeing people create miracles. In feeding the multitude, Jesus asks the disciples not to worry about how limited their resources are, but to commit what they have (the two fish and five loaves) to feeding the hungry. When Peter and the other disciples fear for their lives in the storm at sea, Christ calls Peter to act on faith and come to him, and when the disciples have spent the night fishing without catching anything, they are asked to go into deeper water and cast their nets one more time – once more being asked to act on faith and trust that good things will happen. Thus, for Jesus, **miracles** are **not intended to be** the **cause of faith**, **but** rather the **result of faith**; miracles happen when we commit the resources we have to God and allow the miraculous powers God has entrusted to each of us to create an amazing and wonderful new world. They are not so much what either God or we do by ourselves, but what we do when we allow God's spirit to work within us.

When Little Is Much

Many of us are familiar with the story of Jesus feeding the multitude in the wilderness with five loaves and two fishes, but we may not have seen a recent cartoon that brings the miracle into today's world. In this cartoon, a little girl is looking annoyed at what she has received, and underneath is the caption, "He forgot the tartar sauce." What good is a miracle without tartar sauce!

Where miracles were often an aid to faith for early Christians, in our day they are just as likely to be an obstacle to faith. The problem miracles present for many people is that they violate the laws of nature, which to our scientific minds are inviolable. Like the late Archbishop of Canterbury, William Temple, we ask, "Why didn't God create the world in such a way that it would never need miracles to change it?" In other words, why not do it right the first time? Our modern mind-set has trouble with a God who can change the order of the universe upon a whim. In that kind of a world, nobody can count on anything. It would be nice, of course, if anytime we were in trouble, God could work another miracle, but we know that isn't the way God works.

To be sure, there are some church-goers who resist the modern way of thinking, or at least modify it to read, "Miracles do not happen now, but in Bible times they did". There are also those of a more fundamentalist bent who hold that if you don't believe in miracles, your faith is suspect; to these Christians, miracles are simply a test of faith. But while miracles can be viewed as a test of faith, this approach is too often more concerned with condemning heretics than strengthening our faith, and more importantly, this is not how miracles are presented in the Bible.

In the Bible, there is not just one word for miracle, but several. In Hebrew, the words for miracle, mopheth or pala or eth, mean sign and wonder. In Greek, there are two sets of words: semeion and teras, which like their Hebrew counterparts, also mean sign and wonder, and dynamois and ergo, which mean mighty work. Thus, from the Biblical perspective, miracles are signs of God's power to do great things. Not surprisingly, the Bible is filled with miracles – from the parting of the Red Sea to Christ walking on water, from the manna for the Israelites in the wilderness to this morning's story about Christ feeding the multitudes.

But to Jesus, miracles were of modest importance. To the two blind men whose sight he restored, he said, "See that no one hears about this." Jesus was unwilling to make a demonstration of his healing power; and made this clear when he said to those asking for such a demonstration, "no sign shall be given." And on the cross, Jesus was unwilling to save himself by calling legions of angels to deliver him – for him, private convenience or personal advantage were not proper grounds for a miracle. As the great preacher, Harry Emerson Fosdick, once said, "Jesus never called on his followers to *believe* in miracles so much as to work them; not just believing stories about other people's marvelous deeds; but to manifest God's power at work in their own lives."

As with the blind man whose sight was restored, the key question is not, "How do you explain it?" It is rather, "What does it mean for me?" When pressed as to how it happened that his sight was restored, he simply told his questioners, "Whether he (Jesus) is a sinner I don't know; all I know is that I was blind and now I can see." What, then, do these miracles we read about mean for us? How do we see them with the eyes of faith? How do we allow them to make their claim upon our lives? As we seek to answer these questions, let us take a closer look at this morning's story of the feeding of the multitude with the five loaves and two fish.

One of the first things to note in this story is the background and setting. Jesus has withdrawn by boat to a lonely place where he and his disciples can be by themselves; he has come here to rest. But as he steps ashore, he sees a large crowd has gathered – evidently word about his coming has preceded his arrival. But instead of being dismayed or overwhelmed at seeing them, Jesus takes pity on them and heals their sick.

When evening comes, the disciples, aware of the remoteness of the place, urge Jesus to send the people away so they can return to their villages and find something to eat. But instead of honoring his disciples' request, Jesus tells them there is no need to send the people away, and makes a request of his own, "...give them something to eat yourselves." Since all the food they have with them is five loaves and two fish, their response is one we might, not only expect, but make ourselves, "Our resources are inadequate, and besides, who are we among so many." They assume letting Jesus know the scarcity of their resources will change his mind, and he will agree with their initial suggestion to send the people away. But once more, Jesus' response is not what they might anticipate. "Bring them (the loaves and fish) to me," he says, and then, asking the people to sit down on the grass, he blesses the bread and fish and asks the disciples to give them to the crowd. While they might have had questions about the sufficiency of their resources to feed so many, they do as Jesus asks, and not only is the crowd fed, the gospel story says there are twelve baskets of scraps left over.

Crucial to understanding this miracle story, is the idea of committing the resources we have, regardless of how limited, to God. Instead of questioning the adequacy of our resources, sharing the bread we do have is essential if anyone, much less the multitudes, is to be fed. Whether, as some have suggested, the disciples' act of sharing the little they have serves as a catalyst in evoking a similar response in the crowd, we do not know. Perhaps, their act of sharing was what was multiplied, and in the process, others in the crowd also shared what little they may have had. But whatever the explanation we may employ, the gospel story says it results in the crowd being fed.

A second, and equally important, component of the Biblical miracle is the element of faith – a faith that acts, believing good will come. Just as light is necessary for the vision of the eye, faith is the prerequisite for perceiving Jesus' miracles. Crossing the Red Sea required the faith of the Israelites to first step into the water; so too does feeding the multitude require an act of faith – distributing the resources we have at hand. Faith that what we have will be sufficient is not the cause of the miracle, but it is the precondition. Faith, like a grain of mustard seed, means that <u>little</u> <u>is</u> <u>always</u> <u>much</u> in the hands that commit what they have to God. Thus, miracles are tied to our expectations of what God can do. An expectant openness to the divine possibilities in life is a necessary condition for miracles to occur.

In commenting on this story, William Barclay, the renowned English theologian, has said that in whatever way we approach the miracles of Jesus, one thing is certain: "We must never regard them simply as something which happened once; we must always regard them as something which happens when we allow the power of God to work through us." Thus, miracles are not to be seen as isolated events in history, or something to be believed, but rather they are the current events of our lives when we commit whatever resources are ours to God, and thus discover how little may become much.

Getting Out of the Boat

"He can walk on water," is an expression sometimes used to describe a person, often an athlete or a politician, whose accomplishments seem super-human. Whatever the origin of this expression, the gospel of Matthew's account of Jesus and Peter walking on the Sea of Galilee is surely one of the earliest sources describing such an occurrence.

While this particular, Biblical story is fascinating, it seems more like a fairy tale than an actual happening, and like other miracle stories, raises questions about how it is to be understood. Are we to suspend rational thought, and see it as a test of faith? Are we to understand it in some psychological sense? Or are we to see it as an attempt by the gospel's author to give Jesus divine attributes?

However we may approach this story, any literal understanding violates our ordinary human experience and common sense. Even though the unusually high concentration of salt in Utah's Great Salt Lake makes it easier for a person to float on its water, no one has ever walked on it. And if we approach these miracle stories as tests of faith, do they not become more an obstacle to our faith than something to enhance and strengthen it?

If we are to fully grasp stories like this, it is important to understand that from the Biblical point of view, the emphasis of these miracle stories is upon the **meaning** of the miraculous, not upon the literal act. The miracles are not to be seen as stumbling blocks to our faith, but are rather as **signs of God's saving activity**. Thus, crossing the Red Sea is less concerned with parting the water than deliverance of the Israelites from their Egyptian bondage; feeding the five thousand is less the satisfying of physical hunger than a sign of God's power in Christ to satisfy our deepest needs; and the raising of Lazarus is less the revival of a corpse than the sign of Jesus' power to raise people to new life.

To help us get at the meaning in this story of Jesus and Peter walking on water, it may help to re-visit the story as Matthew tells it. From this perspective, it is good to remember what happens here immediately follows the story of Jesus feeding the multitudes with the five loaves and two fish. Jesus, wanting some time alone for prayer, has sent the disciples back across the lake on their own – a journey that would normally take six to eight hours, but there has been a strong headwind and the choppy seas and high waves have made rowing difficult and the going slow.

Putting ourselves in the boat with the disciples, it may be easier to imagine what they are feeling. Rowing is hard, their hands are cramped, their backs and shoulders ache, and the calming influence of Jesus is no where to be found. The winds are picking up and they are aware that boats bigger than theirs have capsized in these kinds of conditions. They are physically worn down, straining to get to shore, and trying to ignore their fear of sinking.

They've been on the water several hours, and it is now somewhere between three and six in the morning when, across the water, a ghost-like figure emerges. Is it merely their imagination working overtime or some strange creature rising from the deep? What further trouble might this shadowy apparition present? Combating nature's angry sea is stressful enough; they don't need some supernatural threat to add to their fears.

As the shadowy figure approaches, heightening their fears, a voice calls out to them, "Courage, it's me. Don't be afraid." The voice unmistakably belongs to Jesus, but their fears are hardly calmed. The storm continues to rage; the wind still blows and the boat continues to be tossed from side to side. Jesus' presence, always a mystery, has neither calmed the sea nor taken away their fear. Indeed, it has only raised more questions.

As is usually the case, it is Peter's voice that responds. "Lord, if it is you, tell me to come to you across the water." Like the rest of the disciples, Peter is still somewhat uncertain as to what Jesus' ghost-like presence means, but boldly decides to put it to the test. Is he foolish to think he can actually walk on water? Most of us would say "yes". Is he trying to prove something – that he is always ready for a challenge, or that he is braver than the others? Possibly. Is he trying to show Jesus that indeed, he does trust him? Who can say?

Getting out of the boat is never easy. Moving from a place of relative security into the unknown is always frightening. It wasn't easy for the Hebrews when fleeing Pharaoh's soldiers; they had to step into the Red Sea or return to slavery. It wasn't easy for Jesus when he set his face toward Jerusalem, knowing there was growing opposition to what he stood for and increasing anger surrounding his challenge to the authorities.

And neither is getting out of the boat easy for us. Quitting a job with good pension and health benefits to start one's own business that has neither; leaving a marriage that has provided a nice home, but has had a long history of domestic abuse; moving away from one's family of origin and the children's familiar schools to follow a spouse's job relocation in another country; and giving up one's home to move into an assisted living facility in another town are just some of the situations where we may hear a voice asking us to leave the boat.

The church also calls us to leave the boat. Sometimes it is nothing more than giving up a relaxed Sunday morning reading the paper to attend worship; other times it may involve a deeper commitment of one's time and money to support the church's various ministries; and still other times it may mean standing up for a social justice issue in our community in order to make Christ's love more visible to the world..

Whenever the church takes seriously the call of Christ to get out of the boat, it always walks between fear and faith; between concern for neighbor and indifference to neighbor; between openness to God and neglect of God. The church in Paul's day lived amidst the fear of persecution. The church in Hitler's Germany wavered between speaking out against the extermination of the Jews and silent compliance. Issues of race, war and peace, child abuse and prison reform all continue to confront the church, urging we who claim to be Christ's followers to get out of the boat and walk to where he is calling us.

Unless we leave the boat, and like Peter, go across the water, we may never find the hand God offers when wind and wave start to take us down. We may feel safer in the boat, but only in the deep are we likely to discover the love that will not let us go. But if we are to leave the boat, we first have to act on faith. We know the forces to which we are not equal are against us, but the Christ we seek to follow is out there in the storm too, and his hand reaches out to us. If we act on faith and reach out to take it, the same grace that was Peter's can be ours, for it is on such faith that God builds the church. It is safer, of course, to stay where we are, but the voice of Christ continually calls us to come and join him that we may discover that place where miracles truly happen and all our fears are put to rest.

The Last Word

It was every fisherman's dream – not only do you catch your limit, you nearly swamp the boat with your catch. As Luke describes it "their nets began to split" it was such a big haul. Given the fact that the disciples had fished all night without having caught a single fish, the full net that results when Jesus' tells them to put out into deep water seems rather miraculous. Was it just luck, or were other less obvious factors responsible?

One approach we might find helpful in understanding this miracle story is to see it in the context of our dreams. While we're not all interested in catching the biggest fish, and we certainly don't want to swamp our boat, all of us do have our dreams. In our confirmation class, one of the boys said his dream was a Mercedes sports car with the latest built-in speakers and a boom box. For someone aspiring to have a career in politics, their "big" dream may be becoming a U.S. Senator or President. For a twenty-year-old just beginning to date seriously, the dream may be finding the perfect mate. For most parents, the thing they most want in life may simply be the happiness of their children. And for someone trapped in an unhealthy relationship, the dream may be the courage to end the relationship so they can begin life anew.

Luke's story of Jesus and the disciples, which we've just read, can help put our search for dreams in context. Taking a closer look at Luke's account, two things in the story stand out: first, there is **a night of futility** – the disciples, who have been out in their boat all night fishing, haven't even had a bite; and second, there's **a voice asking** them to **give it one more try** – the voice of Jesus telling them to put out into deep water and cast their nets one last time.. Let us now get inside the story by examining both of these aspects in more detail.

If the disciples have been out all night and caught nothing, they have probably not spent the night in one place; most likely, they have cast their lines into different parts of the lake, fishing near the shore and further out, while putting their bait near the surface and letting their lines drag near the bottom. But nothing has come of their efforts. All through the night, they keep hoping their luck will change, but morning finds them empty-handed. Now, as dawn breaks, they're tired, hungry, and disappointed, and simply want to go home, have a bite to eat, and get some sleep.

Have we too not had feelings of exhaustion and disappointment when our hopes and dreams have gone unrealized? Perhaps, it was something that now seems fairly insignificant – like a part in the high school play that we didn't get, or not making the final cut on the basketball team. Or maybe, our disappointment has come in failing to gain admittance to a certain college or not getting hired for our dream job after being interviewed for the second time as one of two finalists.

Still other times, the dashing of our dream may involve a relationship – it may be a divorce, or the break-up with someone to whom we've been engaged, or it may be a father-son or mother-daughter relationship where the son or daughter never quite lives up to the parent's expectations. The adult child keeps going home for the holidays, hoping this time he or she will gain their parent's acceptance, but each new visit is no different from all those that have gone before – the wall between parent and child remains intact, and each succeeding visit only brings more disappointment and heart-ache.

So what happens when our dreams are not fulfilled, and our best efforts are not good enough? Do we just go home and try to forget about it? Do we say, "Enough is enough", cash in our chips and bury ourselves in our favorite snack? After all, why keep coming back for more if it feels we're simply butting our heads against a brick wall? Why not just give up the dream?

Or do we hear that voice urging us to try once more? Does that voice of Jesus that called out to the disciples, *"Put out into deep water and let down your nets for a catch,"* also call out to us? Do we listen to, or even hear, the voice that says, *"Give it another try"*? Or do we give way to our disappointment? Should we quit now or give hope another chance? Is that voice of encouragement worth hearing, or is it just calling us to another futile effort and dashed dream?

Like the disciples, we might want to question the wisdom of this voice of Jesus; the one asking us to give it another chance. After all, what does this Jesus know about it anyway; fishing is not his occupation. He hasn't experienced our night of futility. He can't possibly appreciate what we've been through - neither the efforts we've made nor the disappointments we've experienced.

As we wrestle with our response to this suggestion of Jesus, the one asking us to "give it another try", the key issue facing us becomes clear, "**Who or what will have the last word in our life***?*" Do we, after experiencing our times of futility, reel in our fishing lines and return home, trying to forget our disappointments? Or will that quiet, haunting voice guide our response? Will our future direction in life be more a matter of our **past history** or will it rather be shaped by responding to the **voice of Jesus?** To which of these two, our past history or the call of Jesus, will we give ourselves?

When deciding who will have this last word, two factors seem crucial - "trust" and "risk". Who will we trust more – our past history or that voice that calls us to believe in a different future? Will the failures of the past determine our future? Or will we risk being made a fool for Christ's sake? Yes, indeed it will seem foolish if we, like the disciples, put our nets out one more time and catch nothing for people will wonder why we've listened to an itinerant preacher when we've already tested the waters and caught nothing. And if, on the other hand, we do catch something, people may still see us as fools, thinking we don't know as much about fishing as this inexperienced Jesus.

But before we make our choice, we should be clear what's at stake. In the big picture, it is not just whether we catch some fish or our dreams are realized that's at stake; **it is really a matter of who we will become**. Bringing home a boatload of fish would certainly be satisfying and may enhance our standing in the community, but what if we are being called to something more? What if we are being called to a much bigger purpose – to use our life as a vehicle through which others may discover the miracle that happens when we put our trust in this One who calls us to put out into deeper water, and cast our nets one more time - even when we are tired and have caught nothing?

We may ask why Jesus doesn't just leave the disciples alone after their night of futility. He is surely aware of their exhaustion and disappointment. Why doesn't he just leave well enough alone? Couldn't he just offer some words of encouragement and say, "better luck next time." Perhaps, it has something to do with Christ calling us to an ever higher level of living – a place where we truly experience the fullness of life God intends for us – a place we can only truly discover by putting out into deep water one more time?

Jesus: The Christmas Story

"There is something in me, yearning for a world to be reborn to kindness." Dorothy Brown

Christmas itself is a story and as such invites us into a season that abounds with marvelous tales. Like the incarnation, good Christmas stories are full of deep emotions and mystery. They speak of unexpected joy interrupting the lives of common folks and the excitement of giving. They provoke a sense of awe, wonder, and appreciation. This season, more than any other, seems to encourage us all to be storytellers.

The primary story of the Christmas season, of course, is found in the gospels of Matthew and Luke. Though there is great beauty in reading the Christmas narrative, telling it, when done well, is even more effective. But whether read or told, the greatest obstacle in communication is often the story's familiarity – something not easily overcome even when we try.

One attempt to overcome this familiarity is Megan McKenna's, delightful children's story, "Everybody Knows What a Dragon Looks Like." Using this story to show things are not always what they seem or we imagine, the first sermon in this section seeks to warn us to be careful when we think we know God's holy presence and how it may be revealed. As the sermon, "The Wonder and Mystery of Christmas," explains, the Christmas story can become so familiar we lose sight of the mystery it contains.

The second sermon, "Participants in the Drama," focuses on the typical Sunday School Christmas pageant and suggests the lack of rehearsal time usually evident in the somewhat confused and bewildered children who perform it, is possibly a better indication of our own response to how God is with us than the more professionally produced television productions.

The final sermon, "Dan's Rescue," tells the story of a memorable Christmas when our family decided to go skiing and found ourselves stranded on Crystal Mountain. The resulting experience offered both a deeper appreciation of the kindness of friends and new insight into what Christmas is all about.

The Wonder and Mystery of Christmas

We all know what Christmas is about – shepherds, angels, wise men, Mary and Joseph traveling to Bethlehem, a crowded inn, and a baby born in a stable, wrapped in swaddling clothes and lying in a manger. Yet, Christmas is such a common part of our lives we often forget the mystery and the warning that it hides – in a world with God, we can never know what will happen!

The wonder of Christmas is familiar to us all; it lies in the faces of little children, with their bright eyes and letters to Santa as they eagerly count the days. We hear it in the beautiful carols that are sung, and we see it in the glow of candles and colorful lights that transform the darkest, coldest time of the year into one of warmth and good cheer. We delight in the gaily wrapped packages and the spirit of generosity that transform us all, drawing us closer and encouraging us to extend a helping hand to those in need.

Now it's all right to get carried away by the spirit of Christmas…to eat too much, stay up too late, and even spend more than we can afford, but we need to be careful that it doesn't become so familiar that we lose sight of the mystery that it contains. The danger is that the routine of Christmas may dull our sense of wonder and we will lose sight of the mystery so that we do not recognize the divine presence when it comes.

Megan McKenna has much to tell us about the mystery of Christmas in her delightful children's story, "Everybody Knows What a Dragon Looks Like." The story is set in China in a tiny unknown kingdom that is about to be overrun by warlords from a neighboring kingdom. The army isn't really prepared to fight, the people are afraid, and the wise men of the kingdom counsel the Mandarin to seek help from the Dragon that protects the kingdom. So off they go to seek the dragon's help.

Meanwhile, a small, very poor boy sweeps the gate at the entrance to the city, as he always does in exchange for a cup of tea and some rice. As he does so, a visitor arrives, asking to be taken immediately to the Emperor. The visitor is a short, fat, bald, old man. The boy is willing enough, but warns the old man that the emperor and his counselors are very busy begging the dragon to save them and might not have time for him. The old man nods knowingly and informs the boy that he is a dragon and is here to answer the kingdom's prayers.

The boy looks in amazement at him since he doesn't look like a dragon, and everybody knows what a dragon looks like. Speaking his mind, the boy tells him so. In response, the short, fat, bald, and patient, old man asks him, "How do you know what a dragon looks like? Have you ever seen one?" With the obvious answer, they go off to the Emperor's palace. Unfortunately, the emperor is sure he knows what a dragon looks like and it's not this old man, so he sends him away without even an offer of hospitality.

The man goes off sadly, telling the young boy that he doesn't care much for the city. They are rude, stubborn and unfeeling for an old man. The young boy then offers him rest in his simple home, a cup of tea and some rice, for he feels sorry for his friend. After the meal, the man tells the boy that for the sake of his simple kindness he will save the city. They proceed to the city gates that are empty now, for the town has fled into hiding. In the distance, the dust of the oncoming army is visible. Suddenly, the short, fat, bald old man turns into the most magnificent dragon the boy has ever imagined! He repels the invading army, and the city is saved. The boy goes to find the emperor and tells him that the dragon will stay and protect them, and they now learn what a dragon looks like – a short, fat, bald, old man.

We all think we know what God looks like, and we are pretty sure we know what kind of God we need. As Isaiah describes him, his name is Prince of Peace, Wonderful Counselor, Mighty God. But instead he arrives as just another child, born in poverty to uneducated parents, in a small, little backwater country held in bondage by a powerful foreign army. God, it seems, decides to dwell among the poor, unwanted, unnoticed folks where no one even suspects his coming.

As the gospels point out, those who should have best understood, failed to recognize him and misunderstood his mission. His family asked him to return home and quit preaching; the townspeople where he grew up refused to acknowledge his power to heal; the scribes and Pharisees were aghast at his friendship with sinners and confounded by his teaching; and his own disciples continuously misunderstood what he taught them and abandoned him when he was arrested.

Twenty centuries later, with the sophistication of computers and modern scholarship we think we have arrived at a new level of understanding. Yet, this child who comes to us at Christmas continues to be a warning to us not to be too sure we know God or God's ways. We need to be careful about our expectations for God, and where we expect to find the divine presence. Like the short, fat, bald, old man who doesn't coincide with our ideas of what a dragon looks like, the gospels show us a God who doesn't always meet our expectations.

We are prepared to find God in church, or in the Bible, and we are prepared for a God who honors justice and rewards righteousness, but not a God who embraces whores and throws parties for sons who have spent their father's inheritance. We think we can wrap God in the swaddling clothes of an impossible ideal like peace on earth, or package him in the Apostles' Creed. But in the Fourth Gospel, John the Baptist announces the breaking in of a stranger, "Among you stands one you do not know" – one who is unrecognized, different, strange. God breaks out of our neat little holy places, because where God is, every place is sacred and holy. Shattering our expectations and predictions, God lives them out in unpredictable ways, bursting our safe, neat propositional statements because how can you possibly package fire and life and love.

"Among you stands one you do not know," and the one who comes at Christmas is still a stranger, not just because we sometimes fail to recognize him, but because we so often fail to surrender our lives to his way of love. The mystery of Christmas is not simply to be found in a God who comes to us as a baby. It's even more to be found in we grown-ups who have forgotten or refused to be children of God.

This child, Christmas, is really a warning that we should be extra careful when we think we know God and his ways. We are warned not to judge others, especially those who are alien to us – the poor, the oppressed, the hungry, the uneducated, the prisoner, the radical and prophetic, and those of a different ethnicity – for God is known to come to them first, even looking like them when he decides to become flesh, being born like us, and struggling to be human in a world where everyone takes for granted what being human really means. Christmas warns us that no person's life is trite – that all life is glorious, for God looks like us when Christ comes to save us. Merry Christmas, and look twice at the unknown person you pass in the street or who sits next to you.... for with Christmas, everybody knows what God looks like.

Participants in the Drama

Once, long ago, the main characters of the greatest story ever told were moving toward Bethlehem – Joseph, on foot, and Mary, pregnant on a donkey, traveling the eighty-five miles from Nazareth. Three wise men, perhaps coming all the way from Persia, are following a star to get there, while some shepherds, on a nearby hillside, follow a voice. God, the creator and director of it all, is there too, traveling the incomprehensible distance from transcendence to immanence – from infinity to the finite.

Today, as strange as it may seem, we too are called to be participants in the drama. We are summoned to take our place; to make our journey to Bethlehem and play our part. What might it mean for us to walk on the stage of history today and read our lines so we too may offer our gifts to that baby named Jesus, born so long ago to make the divine presence known on earth?

William Willimon, a fellow Untied Methodist minister, suggests one place we might look for clues to our response is the typical Sunday School Christmas pageant. This suggestion is made, knowing they are usually cute, often comic, sometimes ridiculous, but rarely what we envision as the way the Nativity really looked. Yet, as Willimon says in his latest book, "We may never fully understand the Christmas story until we have seen it done as only our Sunday School classes can do it."

Sunday School pageants, Willimon points out, are probably a lot closer to the reality of what Mary and Joseph actually experienced than what is usually depicted on our Hallmark theater television portrayals. In the Hallmark version, Mary and Joseph and the shepherds seem so sure of what they're doing, making their entrances on cue, confidently going through the birth experience, and then exiting majestically. Mary believes she is blessed, Joseph is not confused, and everyone is in complete control as the story goes off without a hitch.

In contrast, Sunday School pageants never seem to work that way. Mary, Joseph, and the shepherds never seem to look as dignified or pious, and they certainly are not as sure of themselves. The shepherds usually act as confused and dumb-founded as the sheep. Joseph is quite often embarrassed about standing next to a girl, and Mary seldom looks like one who is blessed among women, especially when she giggles. Parents in the audience try not to laugh out-loud, but usually can't help themselves.

But maybe this Sunday school version is closer to the reality described in Matthew and Luke than we think. Perhaps, what happened on that first Christmas was not as neat and religious as we like to tell it. It is doubtful that Mary looked like the queen of heaven that night; she probably looked more like a rather confused and bewildered sixth-grader who doesn't know for sure what to do with the baby or what her next line will be. Joseph stands to the side, not sure what to think. Shepherds, despite all the talk about "fear not", were most likely as scared as you or I would be. They were all in over their heads, wondering what people like themselves were going to do on the stage of history. There was no time to rehearse their parts, or to strike a sufficiently religious pose, or to act as if they knew what they were doing and how the play would end. It all came upon them and overwhelmed them.

But isn't this how God is always with us? We, like Mary and Joseph, and the others, are busy making plans, paying taxes, falling in love, getting engaged, complaining about the government, entertaining strange relatives from the east, plodding through the everydayness of our lives, and then God chooses us to reveal something of himself to the world – perhaps, to send a card, or read a story, or bake some cookies, or deliver some food; to perform some act of love through us. And we, whether we really like it or not, or have the experience or ability or understanding, get pushed onto the stage of history to act our part. And here we stand, with stage fright, filling roles that are too big for us, wondering what our next line will be, yet doing our best to do what God wants us to do, even when we are not sure of our lines.

Perhaps, like Mary, we wonder why God would bother with one like me? But if we identify with Mary's question, can we also identify with her response?

> *"My soul proclaims the greatness of the Lord*
> *and my spirit rejoices in God my saviour; he*
> *has looked upon the humiliation of his servant.*
> *Let it be to me according to your word that from*
> *now on all generations will call me blessed, for*
> *the Almighty has done great things for me.*

Our challenge in being participants in the drama begins with an **acceptance** – a willingness to take into ourselves the incarnation, and to become a part of God's liberating presence in the world so we too may become God's person in the world. We may think it is nonsense that we could do that. Yet, that's the plan. When Mary says, "Let it be to me according to your word," that's the cue to our response. We, too, are called to respond, "Let it be to me as the Lord wills." Even though others may laugh and call it folly that we should try to be God's person, we are called to be just that.

It is not enough to merely be "going about" for there is nothing redemptive in dither. It is alright to decorate our trees, do our shopping, send out our cards, and entertain our friends and family, but we are called to something far greater. We are called to sow seeds of peace and justice; to do small deeds of kindness, like giving away clothes we no longer wear, playing Santa to children whose parents can't afford to be one, drying a tear here, or hearing a grief there. As Luke reminds us, we are called to the task that Jesus calls all who would follow his way - to feed the hungry, welcome the stranger, care for the sick, free the oppressed, and proclaim this the favorable year of the Lord.

So whether we like it or not, or have the experience or ability or understanding, we are pushed onto the stage of history and called to act our part. If by chance this Christmas season some winged angelic messenger from God should appear, whether it be the angel Gabriel, or an angel like most of the ones we see in our Christmas pageants, with a median age of eight, wearing an old bed sheet over Levis and tennis shoes, I think those first words from the Lord will be the same as those first words that the angel spoke to Mary, "Hail, O favored one, the Lord is with you." And yes, with **you, and you, and you!**

There's an oil painting by Derick Baegert entitled, "Luke Painting the Virgin and Child." In it, Luke sits before the easel, painting the portrait of Mary and the infant Jesus. I'm not aware of any other nativity painting where we see the author at work, but when it comes to this Christmas story, aren't we all painters – not just with brushstrokes, but with our lives. What kind of picture will we present to the world as we take up our brushes and act out our parts?

Dan's Rescue

It is our first Christmas at Light of the Hill. We have been a worshipping congregation for only five weeks, and with the demands and pace of starting the new church, I breathe a sigh of relief following our Christmas eve service – tomorrow will be my first day off in six months.

We are not flying back to Kansas to be with our extended family during the holidays so Pat and I decide to take the kids skiing. Twelve-year-old Mark and nine-year-old Jennifer don't need to be convinced. Up early Christmas morning, they have already emptied Santa's "goodies" from Grandma Goering's hand-knit Christmas stockings, and carried their skis to the car. Pat and I decide to skip a nice breakfast and settle instead for a bowl of cereal, a glass of orange juice, and a cup of coffee.

An hour and half later we arrive at Crystal Mountain. It is a beautiful, sunny day and nearly perfect for skiing. As we pull the car into Crystal's parking lot, we see only a handful of skiers – it appears most people have either not arrived or are staying home with family. We join the line for lift tickets, and a few minutes later, are sitting in the lift chair, marveling at the snowy surroundings as we're carried up the slope.

Several runs later, with my legs beginning to tire, we convince the kids to take a break for a slice of pizza and some hot chocolate. Pat and I are already beginning to feel some sore muscles and tired legs, but the eagerness of Mark and Jennifer to return to the slopes makes us glad we have come. I'm enjoying the cafeteria's warmth, but the kids are already making their way back to the chair lift, having agreed to meet us at the Queens' chair lift at three o'clock.

The afternoon passes quickly. Shortly before our scheduled meeting time, Mark and Jennifer appear and inform us that the ski operators are closing the lifts at three. Pat and Jennifer are ready to call it a day, but Mark convinces me to take the lift to the top so we can make a final run down Green Valley. Several minutes later, when we get to the bottom, Pat and Jennifer are waiting outside for us. "They've already closed the cafeteria," Pat informs us. Remembering it's a long ride back home, she suggests we hit the rest rooms before heading to the car. When we come out, the parking lot's empty - people have scattered like kids on the last day of school. We trudge toward the parking lot, summoning our tired, aching muscles to endure for a few minutes more the discomfort walking in ski boots always seems to entail.

By the time we get to the car, everyone is exhausted. We fasten our skis on the ski rack, take off our boots, and get in the car. Shivering, I'm anxious to get warm and head for home. I take off my gloves, fish the car keys from my pocket, and turn the key in the ignition. The engine fails to turn over. The dull click doesn't sound encouraging. I try again with the same result. Don't tell me we have a dead battery! I turn the knob for the lights – my fears are confirmed. It's getting colder and will soon be dark; this is not how the day is supposed to end. Pat senses my anxiety, but like me, is trying to remain calm, not wanting to alarm the kids. Remembering she has put a ham in the slow cooker; I can taste it in my mind, but fear nothing but a charred pan may remain by the time we get home.

What do we do now? There is no spare battery, and I'm no mechanic anyway. Looking around for help only heightens my despair – no one is in sight. We seem to be completely alone on the mountain! I turn to Pat, "Do you have any money for a phone call?" Between us, we come up with two quarters and one thin dime – not much, but hopefully enough to make a call. Surely there must be a phone somewhere. I get out of the car and trudge back toward the ski rental building, looking for a pay phone. Seeing no sign of one, I turn toward the cafeteria, thinking there has to be one somewhere. But it's the same result - my heart sinks. I'm beginning to worry now, not relishing the thought of spending the night on the mountain in a car without heat.

Trying not to panic, I walk around the building, hoping to find an unlocked door. As I turn the corner, I spy a phone booth and quickly approach it. "Please God, let it be in working order." I enter the booth and take the quarter from my pocket, then remember it's Christmas. Who can I call that will be willing to help. With only enough money for one phone call, it's important that it not be wasted. I think first of the Shelton's, since Mary and Beck have been so supportive, but remember they have gone to be with their son's family. The Freeman's live in our housing division, but they left this morning to visit Judy's mother in South Carolina. What about Dan and Cheryl Radonski? Dan and Cheryl have done as much as anyone to help get the church started. I dial the operator for their number, but as I do so, remember I have nothing to write it down. This better not be a time my memory lets me down. I ask the operator to repeat it to make sure I have it right, then thank her, and quickly dial the number. The phone rings once, twice, three times – please, somebody be there.

"Hello." I recognize Cheryl's voice. I don't want to let my panic show or overwhelm her with what now seems a rather desperate situation. "Cheryl, merry Christmas. How are you doing?" I wait for her to answer, hoping we're not interrupting anything important.

"We're just sitting down to eat. What are you doing?" She obviously is in a good mood, but I doubt if she really wants to hear about our predicament. I'd like to be patient and ask what she's fixed for their Christmas dinner, but am already worried three minutes will be up and the operator will ask me to deposit more money. This is not the time to become disconnected!

"Cheryl, we're in a bit of a bind. Pat and I and the kids are up on Crystal Mountain and our car won't start. Could you please call one of those 24-hour wreckers, and see if they could send someone up here?"

"Are you crazy! Dan will be there right away."

"No, No. Go ahead and finish your dinner. If you can just call a wrecker to come and get us, that's all we need." I didn't want to argue, and I certainly didn't want to disrupt their Christmas dinner.

"Don't worry about our dinner. Dan's on his way." I knew she meant it.

"Well, then, please tell Dan to finish his dinner. We're not going anywhere and you should at least enjoy your dinner together." Suddenly the operator's voice cut in, "Your three minutes are up. Please deposit another fifty cents." The phone call ends before I can say "thanks."

Back in the car, I share the good news. Waiting is easier now. A couple hours later, headlights appear; it's Dan, coming to give us a ride home. But more than a ride home, he gives us an understanding of what Christmas is all about – a love that reminds us - wherever we are, even when we're far from home, lonely, cold, hungry and down to our last quarter – we are not alone. We belong to God's family, and there is One who comes to make God's love incarnate! Sometimes the baby Jesus looks like Dan.

"Jesus: The Easter Story"

> *"The empty tomb opens before the world, telling us it is God who still has the last word, not ourselves – on Easter, life looks forward (Godward) toward life, not death."* James Wallis

For the Christian community, Easter is the day the Christian church proclaims the most central tenet of its beliefs, "Christ is risen". Of all the days in the year, none brings more people to church; none calls for greater celebration among the faithful. This is the day the "Hallelujah Chorus" truly resounds!

Since the week of Easter is preceded by both Maundy Thursday and Good Friday services, this is one of the busiest and most demanding weeks in the life of a pastor. For me personally, it always means extra hours preparing an Easter sermon that will present the message of the risen Christ in a fresh and understandable way. I try to wrestle seriously with both the Bible's claim that there is life after death and the reality of the risen Christ, hoping to preserve the mystery surrounding the resurrection while at the same time, taking seriously any doubts people may have about it.

The first of the four sermons included here is based on Paul's words, "If it is for this life only that Christ has given us hope, we of all people are most to be pitied." If the resurrection proclaims there is life beyond death, how does that impact our thinking and the way we live? Does this mean our life on earth is only a prelude or training ground for something else? Is this hint of another world anything more than a pie-in-the-sky attempt to soothe our fears surrounding death? What is the importance of a life beyond this one? In seeking answers, can a deeper appreciation for Paul's claim be gained?

How the resurrection story gets told is at the heart of the second sermon. The earliest gospel account of Christ's resurrection ends with the strange conclusion, "And the women fled from the tomb for fear and astonishment had come upon them; and they said nothing to anyone for they were afraid." How then, if they remain silent, does the story get told? What these women fear and how they deal with their fears is obviously a crucial component of the resurrection story for their response determines, not only how the story gets told, but even if it gets told. And ultimately, does not each person's response to the story, including our own, equally bear upon its continuation?

For those who want more than a faith based on hearsay, the story of the doubting Thomas has great appeal. The desire for a concrete personal experience on which to base our religious faith is the driving force of my third sermon. What role can honest doubt play in our having a vital sense of the risen Christ? Can it enable us to know something more of this risen Christ's transforming power? Can the encounter Thomas has with Christ's wounds, open our eyes as it did his, so that we too may see Jesus in a whole new light?

Of all the accounts of the resurrection, the Emmaus story is my favorite. It is so ordinary and common on the one hand; yet, so strange on the other. The disciples meet Jesus in a stranger, but do not recognize him until they share a meal. He does not impose himself upon them nor come from on high; he simply meets them along the road they are traveling. What role do our expectations play in meeting the risen Christ? Do they sometimes limit what we see and prevent us from a deeper sense of Christ's real presence? May the strangers we encounter today be inherent bearers of the risen Christ?

"If For This Life Only..."

It was a shock to the family, but the real tragedy didn't occur on the night of the accident. That was a year ago, and while it left him paralyzed from the waist down, his life had been spared. The greater tragedy occurred last week when he tried to take his own life. The note he left said, "I have nothing more to live for."

It is understandable why someone who has lost their job and ability to walk might consider taking their own life. Times of despair can make any of us question life's meaning – losing our job, divorce, death of a loved one, loss of a home, a life-threatening illness can all make us question our future life's worth.

And even without any of these personal setbacks, a gray malaise seems to have settled over our world. When hard work may be less important than cheap labor abroad, and one's dream home may be unaffordable and choice of college unavailable, the American dream may seem far less attractive than it once was. When every hope for peace seems derailed by a terrorist bomb and walking the streets of one's own neighborhood may seem unsafe, the future may indeed seem less desirable than the past.

Yet, it is precisely here, in the midst of these times of despair and social malaise that Easter, with its emphasis upon resurrection and eternal life, asks all of us where we find life's meaning. Where and in what do we place our hope? How much of our hope is placed in this life? How much in something beyond this life?

In Paul's letter to the Corinthians which we read this morning, he makes the rather startling statement, "If it is for this life only that Christ has given us hope, we of all people are most to be pitied." What is Paul driving at? Is he suggesting this life is not all that important? Are we to see it as only a dress rehearsal for the main event?

Whatever his meaning may be, what's wrong with putting our hope in this life? Why should we not hope for things here? This is where we live, and is it not what God has given us? And further more, according to the creation story in Genesis, God has proclaimed it good.

Certainly, Paul does not disparage the life we have. He is not saying that this life is of no value. He understands that this world is God's creation and it is to this world that Christ has come. He may not have been familiar with John's assessment of this world's value in God's eyes, "For God so loved the world that he gave his only son...", but he would not have disagreed with it.

How, then, are we to understand Paul's meaning? The key may be in his use of the world "only." We are to be pitied, not when we love this world, but when we hope for nothing more. When we hope for nothing more, the problem is that all our longing is earth-bound.

"So what is wrong with that?" we may ask. "After all, this is home. This is where we live. We know this world exists. Sure, people talk about heaven, but we don't know anything about it – where it's at, what it's like, or even, if it exists, whether we'll ever get there. So why shouldn't we pin all our hopes on the life we have here?"

The difficulty with this view is that if we pin all our hopes on what we have here, if there is nothing beyond this life, then we try to make a utopia out of this present world. If, as the saying goes, "We only go around once," then we better grab all we can get the first time because there won't be a second time. When this attitude is adopted, life can very easily become a selfish cycle of "grabbing" what we can get and pressing on toward some kind of utopia where we will finally have it made. When we are in the grips of this kind of hope, we tend to vacillate between illusion and despair; the illusion that one more acquisition, thrill, or experience will complete our life, and the despair when we realize it doesn't. When we attain a portion of our utopia, we too often discover there is one more hill to climb, one more thing to acquire, one more thrill to experience, and the deeper reaches of our soul remain unsatisfied.

There is, of course, nothing wrong with pursuing the American dream of material success and well-being, unless we let it blind us to the transcendent. When our whole life is centered in "making it", it can keep us from fulfilling an even deeper longing – to connect with something eternal and live in harmony with that which is eternal and of enduring value.. Pursuing the American dream is fine so long as we see it for what it is, and realize that in many ways it's like an artificial apple, aesthetically pleasing, but in the long run not very nourishing.

When we lose sight of the transcendent, we tend to see only what we can measure. Like the child in the cartoon who is looking at the stars in the sky with his father, and asking, "Which ones did we put up there?" We tend to see and value only what we have made, and lose sight of life's creative forces that transcend us.

Perhaps, Edmund Fuller, in his book, "Man in Modern Fiction," is correct when he says, "The new gullibility of our time is not, believing too much, but too little. We've lost our sense of miracle; believing that creation is automatic or commonplace, we think we've seen it all." As he observes further, "This loss of wonder, awe, and any sense of the sublime is a condition that leads to a death of the soul."

This death of a soul is captured rather well in a boyhood memory of the great, French novelist, Andre Gide. In his autobiography, "If It Die," Gide describes a time as a school boy when during one of his math teacher's rather boring lessons, a privet hawk-moth, which Andre had reared and carried with him to the class in a narrow, uncovered box, chose to come out of its chrysalis. Overwhelmed with the beauty of its great, green and pink wings, and nearly dancing with enthusiasm, Andre grabbed his teacher's hand, and pointing at the quivering wings, exclaimed, "Oh, Monsieur Tabourel! Look!"

As Gide notes, his teacher's response hardly shared his enthusiasm for one of the mysteries of life: "*Monsieur Tabourel was a man of education, and calmly, but with a shade of disapproval in his voice, answered, "What! Don't you know that a chrysalis is the envelope of a butterfly? Every butterfly you see comes out of a chrysalis. It's perfectly natural."*

At that Andre dropped Monsieur Tabourel's hand. "Yes indeed," he writes, *"I knew my natural history as well, perhaps better than he...But because it was natural, could he not see that it was marvelous? Poor creature! From that day, I took a dislike to him and a loathing to his lessons."* The death of a soul may occur whenever this world is drained of its wonder and beauty simply because we can explain it.

Many people today criticize the church for something it often has trouble explaining - its otherworldly stance. Talk of another world is condemned as nothing more than "pie-in-the-sky." Often embarrassed by this criticism, and more than a little reluctant to confront it, the church fails to claim one of its major tenets of faith. If we in the church are to truly celebrate the Risen Lord this Easter, we need to once again acknowledge our faith in the resurrection. Having faith in the world to come may no longer be a luxury; it may, in fact, be the one thing that can free us from boredom, disillusionment, and despair when this is the only world we know. It may also be the one thing that can give us hope when a loved one's life is tragically cut short by disease or death.

If there is no life beyond this earth, what can we say to those parents who lose a child or to anyone whose life is tragically cut short by an accident or disease or a drunken driver? If God is dependable and just, why would we be awakened to an awareness of eternity if it doesn't exist? Doesn't it seem a bit unthinkable that God would perfect a mind like Plato's or a spirit like St. Francis only to throw them away like leaves in the wind?

Perhaps, it is only when we are securely grounded in the next world that we may have the strength and tenacity to live faithfully in this world. If we are confident that Christ's resurrection opens the door to another life, then we can be free from the illusions and disappointments of this world for while they may not disappear, they are not all there is. When we see this world against the backdrop of eternity, the highs and lows are put in perspective: when some victory is won, we do not confuse it with the coming of the kingdom; when some defeat is experienced, it is not the end of the world.

When Jesus gave the disciples the power to heal, they exulted in that power, "Lord, we healed diseases; we cast out demons; we did all kinds of marvelous things." But Christ put that in perspective by saying, "Don't ever get so blinded with the things of this world that you lose sight of the world which is to come." For followers of Christ, our real hope extends beyond that which is seen even into the world of the unseen.

A.E. Houseman's poem, "When I Was One and Twenty" speaks to our morning's search for meaning beyond this world. "When I was one and twenty, a wise man said to me, give pounds, and crowns, and guineas, but not your heart away. But I was one and twenty; no use to speak to me. When I was one and twenty, I heard him say again, the heart out of the bosom was never given in vain; Tis paid with sighs a plenty and paid with endless rue. Now I am two and twenty, and oh, 'tis true, 'tis true." If there are some things we cannot know at one and twenty, is it not just as likely there are some things we may not know at one hundred? The glory of the resurrection is that those things that may ever be incomplete and a mystery in our lifetime on earth, may one day be fully revealed.

Sometimes people say to me that the essence of Christianity is to be found in Christ's teaching and the noble example of his life and death. If that were the case, if Christ were only a worthy example, we would not be here this morning, for Christ's death left his disciples sorrowful and defeated. It was their experience of the risen Christ that convinced the disciples that death could not contain him, nor could his embodiment of God's love be contained by the boundaries of this world.

What we celebrate at Easter is not just Christ's victory over death, but the promise that beyond the brokenness and incompleteness of this world there is a wholeness that awaits us in the world to come. For out there is a world where we shall discover the fullness of God's love, and know that peace which this world can neither give nor take away – a peace that in this life we have barely glimpsed.

What it is that God calls us to beyond this life, we do not know; but trusting that there is a power in God's eternal love to renew and restore all things, let us walk confident and unafraid. And let us, with Paul, affirm that "When our earthly tent is destroyed, we have a building from God – not made with human hands, but eternal and in the heavens".

“If The Song Is To Continue,....”

It is now Saturday night. The Sabbath has ended, yet their heads are still spinning from the events of yesterday. Their feelings have run the gamut from fear to anger to disbelief. Things have happened so fast, it all seems unreal; sorting it all out is not easy.

Less than twenty-four hours ago, their friend, Jesus, who always worked for the good of others – healing the sick, embracing the outcast, standing up for the poor, forgiving any who wronged him – was nailed to a cross; put to death as a common criminal. It happened so quickly it all seems surreal – the false accusations, the hurried trial, and Pilate’s capitulation to the mob; it had been a total farce. Still, if someone as good and innocent as Jesus can be put to death so easily, where is justice? And who, if any of us, can be safe from suffering a similar fate?

The question hangs in the air, leaving his followers torn between fear for their own safety and a desire to care for their deceased friend. It is true Jesus is gone, dead and buried; yet he has been placed in a tomb without even a proper anointing of his body. If we can perform this simple act, anointing his body for burial, perhaps some dignity can be given to this senseless tragedy.

And so, early the next morning, spices in hand, the two Marys and Salome set off for the tomb. It isn’t until they are on their way, however, that they think about the large stone blocking the tomb’s entrance. How can three women possibly move such a large stone? Who can they ask for help?

As they climb the last few yards of the rocky hillside, leading to the tomb, they look up and see that the stone has already been rolled from the entrance. If one word can be used to describe the women’s feelings, it would undoubtedly be AMAZED, though the English word is a poor substitute for the Greek (ekthambromai), which has connotations of both wonder and terror. Their amazement might have been similar to what you or I would feel, returning home from a month’s vacation and finding the front door of our home wide open. It is not surprising they approach the tomb with a bit of apprehension. Little do they know what to expect.

Cautiously entering the tomb, it takes a while for their eyes to adjust to the darkness inside. When their eyes do adjust, they see a young-looking man, seated on the right-hand side, wearing a white robe. The young man, seeing their frightened faces, says, “Do not be amazed. You seek Jesus of Nazareth, who was crucified. He has been raised. He is not here. See the place where they laid him. Go tell the disciples and Peter that he is going before you to Galilee. There you will find him as he told you." At first dumbfounded, then trembling with fear, the women flee from the tomb.

Three weeks ago last Tuesday I was turning out the lights to go to bed when the phone rang. A voice on the other end asked, "Is this Mr. Smith?" Hesitating a bit, not sure who is calling or what it is about, I answer, "Yes." "Are you Mark Smith's dad?" My heart beginning to pound, I give a more cautious, "Yes." The caller continues, "I don't want you to be alarmed, but Mark was in an accident – he was hit by a car while riding his bicycle and has been taken to the hospital." Dumbfounded, trembling with fear, like the women fleeing from Jesus' empty tomb, my heart is pounding.

"Do not be amazed….he is going before you to Galielee. There you will find him as he told you." At this point, the entire gospel of Mark reaches its rather strange conclusion for the earliest manuscript of Mark ends with the words, *"And the women fled from the tomb for fear and astonishment had come upon them; and they said nothing to anyone for they were afraid."* Whether Mark intended to end his gospel in this way or whether the ending was torn away and lost, is not known. What is known is the women depart in fear.

Their flight is hardly what we might expect. There is no shout of victory, only astonished silence; no leap for joy, only running in fear. Apparently they have either forgotten or simply not believed Jesus' earlier words to them which foretold of his suffering, death, and triumphant return.

Is their fear simply a holy awe? In the Biblical tradition, a frequent response to being in the presence of God or one of God's messenger's is a similar kind of fear. This was certainly a part of Adam and Eve's response when God called to them in the Garden of Eden where they were hiding among the trees after eating the forbidden fruit. Or does their response arise from the threat of persecution for their association with Jesus. Hearing that Jesus is no longer in the tomb can only mean his enemies will intensify their search, not only for Jesus, but for his followers as well since they may be suspected of having removed his body from the tomb.

Or perhaps, the women fear because of what they have been asked to do. To tell the disciples that Jesus will meet them in Galilee is filled with potential pitfalls. Their message would very likely have been discounted, possibly even laughed at or mocked since women of that time were considered unreliable witnesses. Furthermore, delivering such a message is an uncharacteristic role for women; in the tradition of Israel, men, not women, were called to be divine messengers - telling the disciples that Jesus has risen is not likely to be believed.

Whatever the reason for their fear, the women flee and say nothing to anyone. They have been given incredible news to share – Jesus, who has been crucified, dead, and buried, has risen from the grave. But what will they do with it? If they are silent, what will happen to the story? Will it simply be forgotten – lost in time?

Their silence only adds to the mystery of the resurrection, for it leaves us wondering if the story will ever be told. Perhaps, this was Mark's intention; perhaps it was part of some larger plan. Who knows? Whatever the case, this ending effectively leaves the outcome up to the reader. Mark's account of Jesus' exit from the tomb requires that whoever hears this story must give his or her own response. As someone has said, "We not only question the Bible, but it questions us as well."

Mark's ending is important because it reminds us that what happened in Jerusalem some two thousand years ago has a connection with what happens in each one of us today. Ultimately, unless the resurrection happens in us, it remains someone else's story. Hence, we can never prove the resurrection; we can only witness to it. If the story of Christ's resurrection is to continue, we are the one's who must do the telling.

In the early 1920's, the Soviet Union was attempting to stamp out religion. With this aim in mind, a man named Bukharin, a communist party functionary, was sent from Moscow to Kiev to address a vast anti-God rally. For one hour, he brought to bear all the artillery of argument, abuse, and ridicule he could muster upon the Christian faith. By the time he finished speaking, it seemed as if the whole ancient structure of the Christian faith was in ruins. At the end, their was silence. Questions were invited.

A man, sitting near the front who happened to be an Orthodox priest, rose and asked to speak. Permission was granted. Turning around to face the vast assembly, he gave the ancient, liturgical Easter greeting, "Christ is risen!" Instantly, the multitude of people rose to its feet, and thundered their response like the crash of waves against an ocean cliff, "He is risen indeed!" There was no reply; none could be given.

When all argument is ended, the story of the resurrection requires that every listener reflect about his or her own response, for in the final chapter, it is always up to the listener to determine how the story will end. We can pretend we have forgotten the story; we can say we'd like to believe, but it's too good to be true. But in the end, the story remains, and like the empty tomb, it will not go away.

We are not asked to prove the resurrection, but only to witness to it. The reasons not to tell are many. Like the three women in Mark's gospel, we too may have our fears. People may think we're some kind of "religious" nut. We may feel inadequate and ill-prepared; we may be unsure what we do believe. We may feel too sophisticated for the simple-mindedness of the story. The fear that others may misunderstand and be offended is real and in the eyes of many, fully justified.

But in the end, the fact remains: how the story of Jesus' death and resurrection ends is up to each one of us. To tell or not to tell – that is the question with which Mark's gospel ends.

Joan Brocklesby has written a poem that speaks well to this question:

They told me He was risen,
So I left my quiet house,
And climbed the hill.
I found the garden as they said,
Beset with trees,
And there within, the empty tomb.
The stone was rolled away,
Just as they told me.
I looked within and saw the faded clothes,
But there was nothing more.
No broken body; no risen Lord.
And so I came away, back to my quiet house.
Whom do you seek, Sir,
At my silent door?

I like this poem because it rings so true both to Mark's account of the gospel and to my own experience. There is no startling appearance of the Risen Christ – no proof to convince us beyond the shadow of a doubt. There is only the haunting presence at the door – a presence that asks us when the voices of hate seem loudest, will we stand up for love? When the forces of violence and war seem to rule the world, will we stand on the side of peace and justice? When death robs us of our loved ones, will we continue to trust in the power of an eternal love to bring new life?

Like the cover of our morning's worship bulletin says, "He came singing love, he lived singing love, he died singing love. He rose in silence….that we might take up the song." If the song is to continue, we must do the singing.

Aleluia! World without end! AMEN!

"Has It Ever Dawned On You"

Has it ever dawned on you that Easter is a scandal? That anyone should rise from the dead, no matter who it is, is a claim of incredible proportions! Yet, far too often it is a claim that is either glossed over as if it is something people of faith should believe without question or it is avoided altogether.

For this very reason, the story of the doubting Thomas is a welcome addition to the gospel accounts of the resurrection. Thomas is not the kind of man who makes us comfortable; he says what he thinks and questions what he does not understand. He refuses to accept someone else's word without having his own first-hand experience. He is in short, a disturber of the peace.

Hearsay, for Thomas, is not enough; he wants more than a faith based on someone else's beliefs. Since he is not present when Christ first appears to the disciples, he says, "Unless I see in his hands the print of the nails and place my hand in his side, I will not believe." And in this bold assertion, Thomas appeals to us: he expresses a common, human desire to have some concrete personal experience on which to base our religious faith. We wouldn't think of buying a used car simply on the basis of a car salesman's pitch. Why should we ask any less of our religion?

We want to believe the Easter message that good triumphs over evil and there is life beyond death, especially when we read about the twelve-year-old girl murdered in Defiance Park this past week. But if Christ has arisen from the dead, LET THERE BE A CONCRETE SIGN that this is indeed the case. We want to have a vital sense of the risen Lord so we can know something of his transforming power, and not just give it a nodding acknowledgment one day a year.

Is there a way this can happen for us as it did for Thomas? Can the resurrection be for us, not just a memory of what happened to Jesus long ago, but a <u>living experience for us today</u>?

A closer look at John's account of this story reveals a couple of things worth noting. First, this story makes it clear that doubt can play a positive role in our journey to faith. For many people raised in the church, doubt may seem like a sin, but as Frederick Beuchner, one of this country's finest writers and preachers, has said, "Doubts are the ants in the pants of faith." Just as our health is served when the measles come out so too is our faith when our doubts are expressed. It is because of his willingness to express his doubt that Thomas' demand to see the print of the nails in Jesus' hands is met. Christ does not criticize Thomas for his doubts, but invites him to put them to the test. Honest doubt, seeking to know the truth, need never be suppressed; it can, as it did for Thomas, be the foreshadowing of the dawn of an Easter faith.

And just as doubt can play a positive role in our journey to faith, so too can our wounds. As Henri Nouwen, the priest who gave up a teaching position at Harvard to live the last seven years of his life as pastor to people with mental handicaps in the l'Arche Daybreak community in Toronto, Canada, writes in his book, The Wounded Healer, "wounds, when they become openings or occasions for a new understanding, can become a source of healing and deepen our relationship with Christ." When instead of hating or cursing those who have nailed him to the cross, Christ speaks the words, "Father, forgive them for they know not what they do," he makes of his wounds a source of healing that continues to touch people's lives today even as it has brought new life to thousands of people in every land and century who have been weighed down with guilt.

As Nouwen points out, the cross is not the end of Christ's power, but in many ways it is the beginning; through his suffering and death God continues to work. One of the interesting observations someone has made is that God doesn't save us from suffering and death, but rather our salvation comes through suffering and death. When we sift Christ's life down to its essence, what remains is the incomparable, healing power of an unconditional, forgiving love; a love even expressed to those who cheer his death.

According to John's gospel account, it is Thomas' encounter with Christ's wounds that opens his eyes to see Jesus in a whole new light. After touching his wounds, Thomas voices a new relationship with Jesus proclaiming him, "My Lord and my God." Jesus now stands before him as the one in whom he sees God; for Thomas it is no longer death that writes the final chapter in Christ's life, but God. What happened a couple of days ago, seeing Jesus nailed to a cross, is now pushed to the background by what is happening now – this same Jesus is inviting him to touch his wounds where the nails have been driven into his body. An invitation extended by one whose love, not death, is now the ever-present, final consequence of everything that has happened.

What might it mean for us to see God in this way – to see God as the One who, not only judges, but redeems all that happens? Perhaps, Patrick Carroll and Katherine Dyckman point the way in their interesting book, "Inviting the Mystic, Supporting the Prophet." They suggest faith in God is a process, not a static reality; we become trusting, believing, "faithing" people as we wrestle with the "given-ness and crises" of our lives. Being open to God in all that touches us is what the authors call "a radical response to life"; a response that does not pin our experience of God to one place or one event, but thinks and lives continually in God's presence.

If Thomas does not surrender his previous understanding of death, that nailing Jesus to a cross has put an end to their relationship, he can not be open to experience the risen Christ who confronts him now. It is only as he is able to let go of his past picture of Christ dying on the cross that he can allow the living Christ to stand before him, inviting him to touch his wounds. Can it be that we too must surrender our previous understanding that death is the final chapter in our lives before we, like Thomas, can be open to see God also working in the wounds of our life, and in a whole new way.

None of us may have Thomas' experience of touching Jesus' wounds, but like him, we too have our doubts and encounters with life's wounds. And like Thomas, our doubts and wounds may lead us to not only question what we believe, but also open our eyes to see life in a whole new way; a way that not only challenges our faith, but also deepens and strengthens it. Our wounds and doubts my seem like a curse, but they may also deepen and strengthen us so that in our vulnerability we too may experience the mysterious presence and transforming power of God's holy love, and God may truly become for us, as for Thomas, the One who stands before us as our Lord and savior.

Now, Holy and Mysterious God, as we celebrate another Easter, may you who make the stars and can turn the shadow of death into morning, convince us in our very bodies that we live and die in the hollow of your hands, and give us the confidence that though all things change, you are the same God, ever gracious, from whose love nothing in all creation can ever separate us!

"The Road To Emmaus"

Of all the accounts of the resurrection, the Emmaus story is one of my favorites. It has been called one of the loveliest stories in the New Testament, and it definitely is one of the most intriguing for it raises a difficult question: "If the risen Jesus walking and talking with two of his contemporaries is unrecognizable, how are we to recognize his presence with us today? If the risen Christ is a stranger to those who knew him back then, how much more of a stranger must he be to us twenty centuries later?

To gain a better understanding of the story it may be helpful to first ask, "Where is Emmaus?" Geographically, Luke tells us it was seven miles from Jerusalem. In a more universal sense, however, it has been suggested that Emmaus is wherever you go or whatever you do, just to get away. In this sense, Emmaus can be going to the movies or turning on the television just for a distraction; it may mean a shopping spree or drinking more cups of coffee than we really want. It is simply those things we do to make ourselves forget when our hopes and dreams have been dashed.

Two such persons are Cleopas and his companion. Their whole past week has seemed unreal – every time they close their eyes they can see the three men hanging there in the hot sun, the sound of the hammer echoing in their ears. Nothing seems to fit any more; nothing seems right. Once they had been so sure, but now everything is confused - out of joint. They just have to get away; so the two of them set out for Emmaus.

Along the way they have a strange encounter – an encounter with a stranger, who turns out to be Jesus. And if this isn't enough, stranger yet is the fact they do not recognize him – at least, not at first. So what goes on here? This is not a fifty-year, high school reunion. They have been in almost daily contact with Jesus, and furthermore, only three days have elapsed since they last saw him. If this is the risen Christ, why is he so difficult to recognize?

One thing for certain, this stranger seems to be shrouded in mystery. His actions are abrupt, and somewhat contradictory. He suddenly appears, and just as suddenly vanishes; he is at first ignorant, then wows them with his understanding. When it appears he will go on, he stays; and when he appears to be staying for dinner, he breaks the bread, and then leaves. No wonder they do not recognize Jesus.

Numerous explanations have been offered for this failure. Maybe the sun was in their eyes or perhaps they were simply blinded by their sorrow, preoccupied with what it all meant, and unprepared for something that seemed so out of step with their expectations. Whatever the case, this risen

Christ is not tied down by any of their expectations, nor is his reality limited by their perception.

But Jesus had met no one's expectations. For the Israelites who expected God's chosen deliverer to come on clouds of glory, Jesus arrives as just another child, born in poverty to an unwed mother. And when he stirs people's passions and hopes that he will lead a revolution and overthrow their Roman invaders, he comes not carrying a sword and calling for a revolution, but riding on a donkey, preaching peace and asking people to forgive their enemy, and turn the other cheek. The religious people were aghast at his friendship with sinners and his disciples were confounded by his teachings – "... the first shall be last, and the last first", "except you become as a little child you shall not enter the kingdom of heaven", "love your enemies and pray for those who persecute you."

When it comes to recognizing this stranger the disciples met on the road to Emmaus, it is clear his presence points to a mystery that baffles them, yet leaves them filled with awe and wonder, "Were not our hearts burning within us as he talked with us on the road and opened the scriptures to us?" And if Jesus baffled people then, why should it be any different now? If Christ really is the clue to how God acts, God will probably not fit easily into any of our notions either. Our human tendency is to want to domesticate Jesus - to tame him so he conforms to what we think is possible, and how we think God acts. We want him to be the kind of person with whom we are comfortable, not some stranger whom we don't even recognize. We want him to conform to our values and ideals, not challenge them. We want him to be close and familiar, not distant and mysterious; forgiving, not judging; giving us comfort and peace, not asking us to meet him in a stranger.

But let us not get too dismayed, for if Christ is a stranger, there is a strange sort of comfort in all this. Perhaps, when we are baffled by the way God works in the world, he may be closer than we realize. Like Cleopas and his companion whose sorrow blinded them to Christ's presence, we too may find those times of sorrow when we just want to get away from it all are exactly the times when this mysterious stranger walks beside us. So when our prayers seem unanswered, when either we or someone we love battles cancer or some crippling disease, when our marriage is on the rocks and our family is falling apart, when someone we love dies, when we are out of work, or the work we have seems to have lost any meaning – in all these empty places that cry out to be filled – we may meet the stranger on the road.

As the disciples discovered when they walked along the Emmaus road, he is quiet and unobtrusive. He comes and goes without fanfare – so quietly he seems to come out of nowhere and then vanishes into thin air. He comes, not from on high, but in the midst of real life and the questions that real life asks: questions about where the road we are traveling is finally going to take us, about who we are, and who the stranger is that walks beside us.

Jesus does not force himself upon Cleopas and his friend. He appears to be going farther, and only stays when invited to share a meal. Had he not been asked to stay, it seems he would have gone on. Though he walks with them, he does not impose himself upon them. As a result, their recognition of the risen Christ only comes after they invite this stranger to stay for dinner. Ultimately, Jesus is recognized as the risen Christ in the breaking of bread. Breaking the bread together was not a matter of two disciples preparing a sacrament and hoping Christ would be present; rather it was two people offering hospitality to a weary stranger. The risen Christ is recognized only when they share their bread, thoughtfully responding to this stranger's needs.

Where might we meet this stranger today? Perhaps, in that moment when we reach out in empathy to another's need; perhaps when we make room for one whom others ignore or think ignorant. When and where such moments come may not always be announced with bold headlines; more often than not they may appear so quietly it is only in looking back that we recognize them. Only God knows where we will meet this stranger who forever moves beyond the bounds of our worldly constraints. But if we reach out to welcome him wherever he may be, our eyes may be opened to see a whole new world – a world where the transforming power of God's love opens our eyes to see things in an entirely new way.

LaVergne, TN USA
31 January 2010
171647LV00001B/22/P

9 781608 441488